Left Early, Arrived Late

Left Early, Arrived Late

Scenes From The Life of Marcia Muth, Memory Painter

Teddy Jones

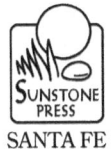

SUNSTONE PRESS

SANTA FE

Sunstone books may be purchased for educational, business, or sales promotional
use. For information please write: Special Markets Department, Sunstone Press,
P.O. Box 2321, Santa Fe, New Mexico 87504-2321.

Book design ⊷ Vicki Ahl
Body typeface ⊷ Century Old Style Std.
Display typeface ⊷ Bradley Hand ITC
Printed on acid free paper

Library of Congress Cataloging-in-Publication Data

Jones, Teddy, 1943-
Left early, arrived late : scenes from the life of Marcia Muth, memory painter / by
Teddy Jones.
    p. cm.
ISBN 978-0-86534-665-9 (softcover : alk. paper)
1. Muth, Marcia, 1919- 2. Painters–United States–Biography. 3. Authors, American-
-20th century–Biography I. Muth, Marcia, 1919- II. Title.
ND237.M94J66 2008
759.13–dc22
[B]

                                    2008023626

Published in

WWW.SUNSTONEPRESS.COM
SUNSTONE PRESS / POST OFFICE BOX 2321 / SANTA FE, NM 87504-2321 /USA
(505) 988-4418 / ORDERS ONLY (800) 243-5644 / FAX (505) 988-1025

Epigraphs for Scenes 14 and 15 are from *Composing a Life* by Mary Catherine Bateson published 1990 by Penguin, New York.

Epigraphs for all other Scenes are from *The Soul's Code* by James Hillman, copyright 1996 by James Hillman. Used by permission of Random House, Inc.

Poetry by Marcia Muth quoted throughout by permission of Sunstone Press, Santa Fe, New Mexico.

Photo Credits: Page 139, Judith Armstrong; Pages 144, 147, and 151, Bob Thompson; Page 155, Jackie Mathey.

Acknowledgments

Thanks and appreciation to each of the people who participated in the interviews that provided different perspectives on Marcia Muth. Each, in his or her own way, has helped to add depth and shading to these scenes. They are: Ms. Judith Armstrong, Ava, MO; Ms. Laurie Carmody of Galerie Bonheur, St. Louis, MO; Mr. Pete Cecere, Woodville, VA; Mr. Willard Chilcott, Santa Fe, NM; Mrs. Mary Lou Colgin and Mr. Jim Colgin, Manilus, NY; Ms. Roslyn Eisenberg, Santa Fe, NM; Ms. Sondra Everhart, Santa Fe, NM; Ms. Marilyn Fisher, Santa Fe, NM; Ms. Mary Jean Kerr, Oradell, NJ (who also supplied copies of correspondence with Marcia); Ms. Gail Kaplan, Santa Fe, NM; Mrs. Florence and Mr. Jules Laffal, Montpelier, VT (who furnished copies of material from their publication, *Folk*

Art Finder); Ms. Kay Lockridge, Santa Fe, NM; Margeaux, Santa Fe, NM; Mrs. Virginia Ott and Mr. Ted Ott, Scottsdale, AZ; Ms. Roslyn K. Pulitzer, Santa Fe, NM; Ms. Gwendolyn Roberts, Battle Creek, MI; and Ms. Betty Carol Sellen, Deale, MD.

Mr. Jim Smith, President of Sunstone Press, Santa Fe, introduced me to Marcia and encouraged her to allow me to tell her story. So, in addition to thanks for sharing his own recollections about and perspectives on Marcia, he deserves a "finder's fee." Carl Condit, Director of Operations at Sunstone displays unerring good humor and kindness. Thanks to him for being Carl.

And to Jody Ellis, thank you for allowing me to ask lots of questions and for interrupting your life of music and joy to give me answers. In the process, you shared with me both music and joy. Thanks also for welcoming me into your home so graciously. You made me feel at ease. Among the many things that you are and do, you really are still a nurse, in many ways.

Marcia Muth permitted me to ask questions that one does not broach in polite circumstances. The answers were always thoughtful and interesting and very often entertaining. She taught me some about art, some about imagination, and a lot about living successfully. By demonstration, not lecture, she taught me things about friendship. She let me look at family photographs; she laughed about her own and others' behavior.

She introduced me to her paintings full of memories and I found myself smiling the smiles those paintings evoke. Drollites danced for me and fish not known in nature swam for me in the waterless aquarium in her studio. And she gave me poems. I thank you, Marcia, for all of that—particularly the poems. I am honored that you have allowed me to show these scenes from your life.

—Teddy Jones

Introduction

Marcia Muth, the subject of this book, permitted me to learn from and of her and to convey my impressions as a work of biography. That she was willing to be interviewed extensively and to provide me with contacts for additional information are remarkable acts of disclosure. Many of us are so concerned about our privacy that openness of this sort would be painful even if everything that resulted was extremely positive. She also is private, but also honest and self-assured. The result is a story of 88 years of the life of a remarkable woman who some have known as an odd child, others as a poet, others as a librarian, others as an entrepreneur in the early days of the Santa Fe literary scene, and still others as a painter.

A Perspective on Biography:

A reader who expects a biography to provide a literal and entirely "factual" account of a life is bound to be disappointed or to be deluded. If the reader accepts a particular written life story as an absolute and undebatable description of how the person led her life, that is a comfortable delusion. If the reader hopes to find only verifiable facts, devoid of interpretations or of omissions (either those of intention or oversight), then any biographical work can only disappoint. It would be information better suited to a biographical dictionary.

Given that pessimistic-sounding notion of biography as a literary form, why would I choose to call this a biographical work? Why not call it fiction and be done with the fine distinctions, not be held to any standard of veracity or accuracy? The answer is that there's a special challenge in working without invented plot or characters. The task is to offer the reader access to a real life and to all the possibilities for wonder, instruction and inspiration a real life offers that a fictional one cannot.

A part of the special challenge to which I refer is that of applying standards of good historical research to the process of gathering and analyzing information and synthesizing an argument or thesis that the information can support or refute. The research upon which a biography is based, a large part of which is related to the history (the events and context) surrounding a particular person, may differ little from the research a novelist undertakes en route to fabricating one person or an entire civilization. I must not only seek data from the subject directly (if living) but also from as many others as are available to be informants about the subject. This particular aspect can be difficult if, as has Marcia, the subject has outlived most of her age-mates and family. The result is that most informants will be younger than the subject. Although age differences are not in themselves predictors of any particular biases, one may find fewer peer relationships and more late-life contacts or friendships, mentor-mentee or parent-child interactions than would be the case were the subject's early contemporaries available for interview. The caution? Simply that I must strive to be aware of the various perspectives from which a person can be viewed and aware that to each person her or his view is entirely valid.

Documents or other material produced by or about the person are fodder for the study as well. And each item must be subjected to all possible verification. In the case of one who gained some public notice rather late in life, the documents about Marcia are fewer than might be the case had she been publicized at an earlier age. And then there's the search for information about the actual individual's context. A person who lives a long life likely has many personal, social, and cultural contexts. Stacks and piles of data grow as each new source tempts the would-be biographer to ask more questions.

Another part of the challenge is to remain aware that regardless of all attempts at verification, in the end all information has been interpreted by at least one human (the source) and often many more. This is true of even such basic data as vital statistics records. The shadow cast by that is offset somewhat by the weight of evidence created when several sources agree. As an example, Marcia Muth was characterized by almost every person I interviewed as having a whimsical way of viewing the world. Therefore, I am comfortable conveying her in that light.

Also, my intention that no plot is to be forced onto a real life creates challenge. Biographies often suggest that some lives seem to have been lived for retelling; waiting for print or film to convey them as inspiration for an audience. Their telling follows the quest theme, a journey toward a fulfillment that defines the person's being. An example: the subject is indelibly and for all his life an astronaut; all of his early life led directly to that, although he was deterred occasionally by conflicts or circumstances. Some skillful biographers discover and portray character flaws that threaten the eventual accomplishment of the quest and make the story even more dramatic. Some tell of the "potentially great person fallen from grace." In each of those cases, the writer is offering a view of a plot of the subject's life and weaving the facts to support that plot. Even though the facts are not inventions and are verifiable, the "plot" is a narrative structure with predictable elements that make for an interesting story. And that structure (this happened, then this, and then this was the result) can encourage the writer and the reader to infer coherence, a clear direction, a reasonableness to a life or portion of a life that was not evident at the time the life was being lived.

A Perspective on This Particular Biographical Work:

My effort to convey Marcia Muth's essence is an effort to avoid the typical overlay of plot and also to avoid explaining her from the perspectives of most accepted theories of human development. Rather, I began with two facts about Marcia Muth that I gained in response to a question I asked her friend Jim Smith. I had seen her sitting with him at a reading I did in Santa Fe. "Who is that little woman who was sitting with you?" He replied that her name was Marcia Muth, one of the two original founders of Sunstone Press. My reply—who knows what caused my interest, perhaps her eyes—was, "I imagine she has an interesting story." He responded that she definitely is amazing and added other items that further piqued my interest. Those were that she was sent away by her parents when she was very young, eventually being brought up by grandparents; that she had become a successful painter after she was 65; and that she was one of the two developers of the first literary magazine in Santa Fe and subsequently of Sunstone Press.

James Hillman's book, *The Soul's Code*, had caught my interest in a similarly unintentional fashion. No student of archetypal psychology, I am a dilettante of a reader. I often think that certain books find me. Sometime between its publication in 1996 and 1999, I bought the book, probably based on its title. I read and reread it, underlining passages I particularly liked. I had on more than one occasion suggested to a patient, a friend or a colleague that its perspective was a beautiful alternative to applying as norms child and adult developmental theories that should be, at best, provisional explanations. Clearly, it had meaning for me.

In that book, Hillman offers the following explanation of his "acorn theory": "The soul of each of us is given a unique *daimon* before we are born, and it has selected an image or pattern that we live on earth. This soul-companion, the *daimon*, guides us here; in the process of arrival, however, we forget all that took place and believe we come empty into this world. The *daimon* remembers what is in your image and belongs to your pattern, and therefore your *daimon* is the carrier of your destiny."

Certainly, Hillman's use of myth to explain humans' course through life runs counter to much that is accepted. He is aware that the ancient custom of explaining and predicting through myth has gone out of vogue. Yet, he makes a rather convincing case that there is as much lacking in the soundness of scientific theories of development and psychology as there is inexplicable in the acceptance of myths.

That became the beacon by which I chose the path for telling Marcia Muth's story. Its thesis became the argument of this biography. That is, that she was accompanied by her *daimon*, the acorn, to become who she has become/is becoming. As interviews with Marcia and more than thirty friends and acquaintances provided facts and impressions, I found little to refute that premise.

Beginning at her current age of 88 and looking back, it seems that no positive experiences were designed by her family to encourage her self-esteem. Developmental theory would suggest that her early distrust of adults should have thwarted her function and movement to later "stages" that those theories convey. Role models in her early family life did little to nurture a sense of artistic or literary talent. Her childhood-continuing-into-adulthood fantasy life could be explained as aberrant behavior by any number of psychological theories. No quest plot can be neatly overlaid showing a singular goal achieved in spite of or because of a lifelong journey toward it. Neither those theories nor that narrative device, the quest, explain why she would succeed and thrive.

Those same features—less than positive role modeling, lack of nurturance of artistic inclinations, early abandonment—together with evidence of a long and successful life do support the argument drawn from Hillman's acorn theory—she was meant to be just as she was and is.

Organization of This Book:

The segments of this book offer stories drawn from throughout Marcia Muth's life, along with inferences about the influence of her accompanying *daimon* that the stories suggest. Indicating the guidance that *The Soul's Code* provided in development of this work, most segments are preceded by an epigraph from that book.

In addition to the narrative about Marcia's life, each segment also contains photographs of Marcia and of places and people from her life related in some fashion to the portion of her life related in that segment. The resulting combinations of narrative and visual material that form the structure of the divisions of the book seemed better characterized as "Scenes" than as "Chapters." It's not a standard biography, but neither is Marcia Muth a standard subject.

Good Fortune:

My good fortune is evident in having been drawn to Marcia Muth and to Hillman's book. Neither of those happened for any reason that I know. I hope that in visiting these scenes, you, as I, will smile with pleasure and nod with appreciation that we humans are fortunate to have our *daimons* choose us.

—Teddy Jones

She's Not Our Responsibility and We've Never Been Paid

The acorn theory . . .says 'Your daimon selected both the egg and the sperm, as it selected their carriers, called 'parents.' Their union results from your necessity—and not the other way around. Does this not help to understand the impossible unions, those antipathies and misalliances, the quick conceptions and sudden desertions occurring between the parents of so many of us, and especially in the biographies of the eminent? The couple came together, not for their personal unity, but to beget the unique person, endowed with a specific acorn, who turns out to be you. Hillman, J., *The Soul's Code*, p. 64

"What they did was rather strange," she said. A tiny smile and not a hint of rancor accompany that understated summary of her arrival on her grandparents' front porch sometime in her sixth year. "I learned later that my (maternal) grandfather's sister and her husband who were older and had not had children had asked to adopt me. They lived in Attica, New York where they had a furniture store and had other interests and a beautiful home. I visited there as a teenager. I didn't know until I was older that they had asked to adopt me. I often wondered why my mother refused to allow them to, but she had said no and they didn't pursue it further. I wondered later why, if they were interested, she wouldn't agree, but I think maybe it was a matter of family pride, somehow.

"Instead my parents found this young couple, some distant relatives, I think, who were willing to take me into their home. They were young and I don't think their lives were too good. Hard times, you know. So, they were supposed to be paid for my being there and I was to help with their baby and do a few chores. That was the year I was in the first grade."

Neither her parents nor grandparents came to visit or to pay for her keep during the several months that she was there.

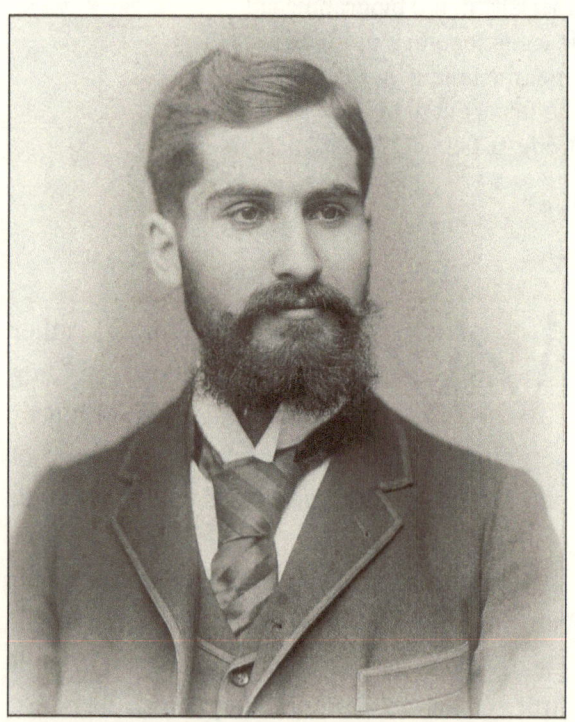

Charles J. Welker, Marcia's Grandfather, Around 1897

"They all lived there in town, in Buffalo, but it was as if they just vanished. I was there; I went to school. I loved school and I learned to read. I didn't give a thought to where they were. I didn't wonder if this would continue all my life, because I didn't think that far. The thing was that my parents' relation to me was so strange that I never missed any of my family when they weren't there because I didn't have any attachment to them, nor did they have one to me, obviously.

When they realized that they had been duped and would never be paid, the couple packed up little Marcia's belongings and took her to her grandparents' home. Asked if she recalled any feelings of anguish or abandonment, she replied, "The only anguish I felt was that I didn't like to push the baby buggy and to clean the toilet. To this day I don't like to clean the toilet. They were never unkind to me." Although she has several vivid memories of her childhood, the name of the couple with whom she lived during that first year of elementary school is not among them. But she does remember that she learned to read and loved it.

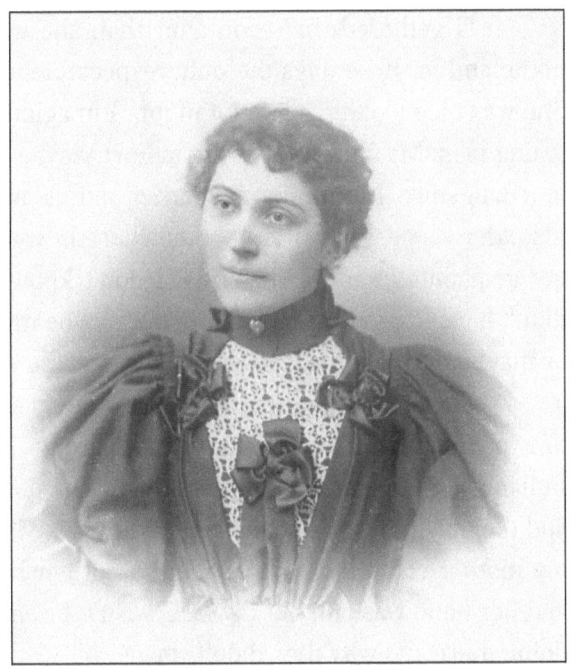

Adeline ("Addie") Welker, Marcia's Grandmother, Around 1897

Since her birth in 1919, Marcia had lived with her parents Margaret Welker Miller and Frank Miller until they decided to divorce. During those five years, they lived in Fort Wayne, Indiana where she was born; Muncie, Indiana and in Buffalo, New York.

"My mother was an interesting person. I didn't know until I was probably twenty-something that she had been married briefly while she was in high school. She said at a meal, and everyone else seemed to know what she was talking about, that she'd been to the bank that day (and had seen someone there), 'Boy, am I glad I didn't stay married to him. He has three children!' Later I asked my aunt who she was talking about. She said, 'Oh, she ran off with him and was married and both families were very upset and they tracked them down and had it annulled.' Grandmother had to go to the Superintendent of Schools whom she knew to get her let back in school. It was quite a scandal and was kept quiet.

"I gathered that soon after that, she was determined to leave home and in those days the only respectable way was to get married. She was nice looking and a lot of fun. I imagine she attracted plenty of young men. My father was living in Fort Wayne at the time and working in a drugstore. I think that my father and his mother lived there while his older sister was working somewhere in vaudeville. Somehow they got acquainted and got married. I don't know why my grandmother didn't have that one annulled too, but maybe my mother was pregnant, or maybe they just realized that she was going to keep doing it."

Recalling those first five years, Marcia says, "They spent a lot of time trying to get away from my grandparents. They moved to Muncie, Indiana at one point when I was a baby. Of course I don't remember it and the only reason I know it is that they were in a taxicab accident and my mother said that she managed to put her hand in front of my face and her hand was cut, but my face wasn't. I don't know what they were doing there and why they didn't stay.

"My father left her one time when they lived in Fort Wayne and I do remember they followed him and made him come back. 'Your daddy is coming home,' they said. He was coming to the train station so we went to meet him. I don't think I'd noticed he was gone.

"After that we moved to Buffalo. We weren't there very long before—guess who appeared? The grandparents. They moved there; my aunt Doris too. My grandmother did not like my father and she intended to watch him."

Frank Miller's return at the train station was mentioned later by Marcia in a poem, "March 5." The title is her father's birthday, which in the poem she says she recalls by the incident at the train station. She was fascinated by the porter's red cap far more than by the return of her father. The poem, published in a collection in 1987 contains these lines:

> . . . And I heard someone laugh in my direction
> As I was wrenched from my mother's arms,
> Swept up by a new stronger force
> Strange father, stranger child; I wept,
> My allegiance defected to a gold-braided cap.

Frank Miller was born in 1901 and Margaret Welker Miller in 1899. At the time of Marcia's birth, they were young, just 18 and 20. He was the son of a family of performers. His father, Marcia's grandfather, was an actor and his mother took tickets for performances. Her aunt Myrtle was a star in the shows, dancing and singing. Frank acted and danced and his brother Lester later became a "wing-walker" in air shows. The family usually stayed a season in a particular place, performing for their living and then moved on to another location. If there was no performing work available, her grandfather Miller would work painting scenes on people's walls in their homes, a popular form of decorative art.

It's not difficult to see the reason for Margaret's attraction to Frank Miller. Photographs show a handsome, dark-haired man. That and his family background made him the perfect choice for her and a perfect way to upset her staid mother's tight control.

However, even the grandmother's effort at continuing control and their parental presence in Buffalo did not assure that the young couple would settle into domestic routine. Frank began to attend college to become a pharmacist. Both he and Margaret found separate interests and other people. The result was a divorce and the "placement" of Marcia with the couple and their baby. The parents agreed to omit any mention Marcia's existence in the legal proceeding for the divorce, thus avoiding any complication that her presence might cause later.

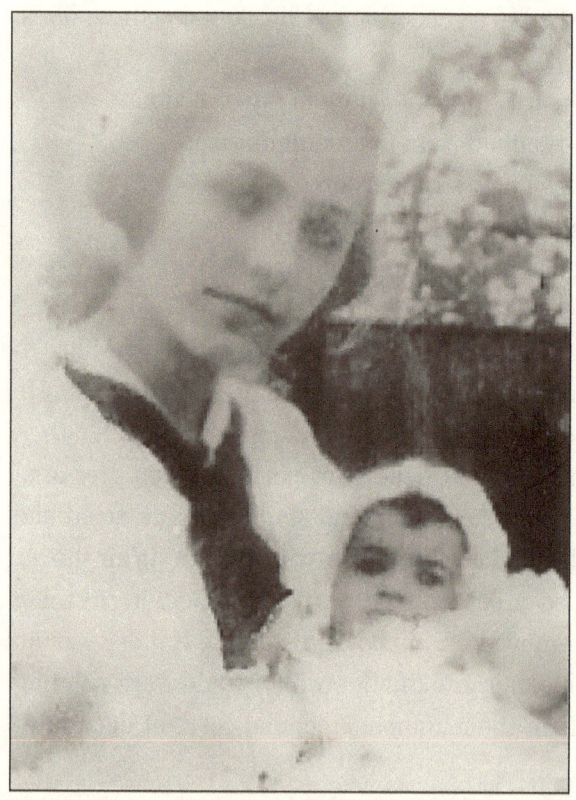

Marcia, Age Two Months with Aunt Doris Bernhardt, 1919

If those first years caused her to resent her parents' behavior, it is long forgotten. "No, I never resented them," she said. In fact, at the age of 88, Marcia seemed both amused by and somewhat analytical about her family and her childhood. "My mother was like a cat that had one kitten and then just left. And that's okay, she was an interesting person. I didn't ever live with her but I did get to know her later—we had occasional meetings because we lived in the same city when I was a teenager. I look back now and I realize I wasn't upset, but they were just not there and I didn't think about them," Marcia said. "My parents were really not suited to be married to each other or to have children."

Adults Are The Natural Enemy of Children—Not to be Trusted

> . . . You are born with a character; it is given, a gift, as the old stories say, from the guardians upon your birth. Hillman, J., *The Soul's Code*, p. 7

A common assertion by anyone telling parts of their life story is, "I was always different." Hardly any of us is eager to declare a dull similarity to almost everyone else in the world. No, we prefer to see ourselves as unique; surely a healthy stance. Otherwise, what's the point of telling— or listening to—the story? Marcia Muth does not make that sweeping claim that many of us would if there were no one alive who could challenge it authoritatively. Although she has no close relatives who could dispute any images of the developing seeds of an heroic quest she might choose to portray from her childhood, she asserts simply, "I was always an observer of adults."

Her retelling of those memories of her first six years offers no stories of deprivation of clothing, food or attention. There are no horrors of punishments or of physical abuse. Rather, she recalls episodes in which the child collects observations of the adults around her. No one in the stories she recounts of those first years is a malevolent character. No one offered harsh or direct opposition to her *daimon*. Perhaps they nurtured it, unwittingly.

An example of an observation which led to her eventual, and quite logical, conclusion about adults describes a gathering at her home. She's not certain of the year, but it was during the first five years because she lived with her parents at the time. "There were some people there, a man and a woman, and my parents. I don't know why, but someone had a gun. It was a real gun but I knew it wasn't loaded. They were all laughing and joking and talking to me. My father handed me the gun and someone said, 'Shoot him.' I pointed it and pulled the trigger. He fell to the floor as if he had been wounded. I looked at him and then went back to playing. I knew he wasn't dead. The others were upset with me, asking, 'Why didn't you try to help him; why did you shoot him; why weren't you afraid or crying?' I said, 'Because he wasn't hurt. I knew he wasn't, so why be upset?' They were upset because I knew it wasn't real and because I didn't act like they thought I should, like a child should. They thought I should be stupid because I was a child."

It's clear that even though she was a child, she was far more observant than adults expected her to be and far wiser than they realized. "My mother entertained male visitors while my father was away from the house, at college I suppose. Afterward, she would always say to me, 'Now we won't mention this, will we?' I didn't. At the same time, my father would let me go with him and we would visit this woman at her place. She was nice to me. She had a little toy washing machine that I liked to play with. While I did that, they would go into another room. And later, he would say, 'You don't need to tell your mother about this.' You can see why I would think that adults were strange. It didn't worry me; I just knew better than to believe things they said.

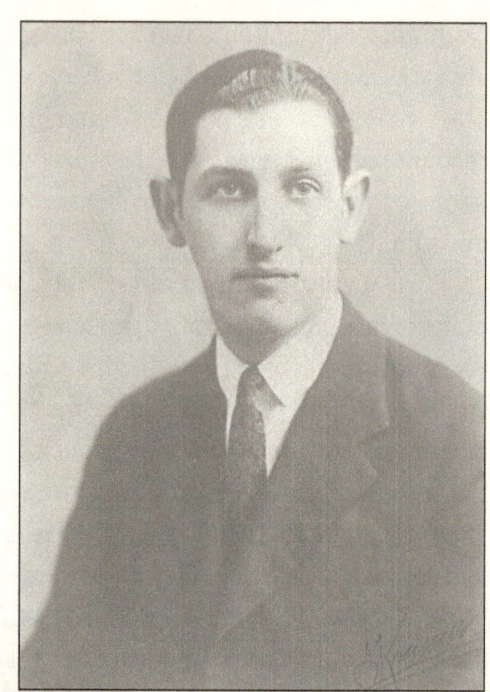

**Frank O. Miller,
Marcia's Father, 1920**

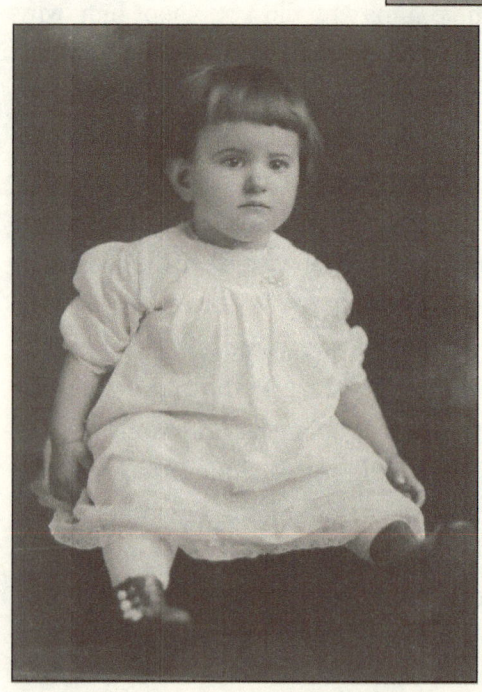

Marcia, Age Two, 1921

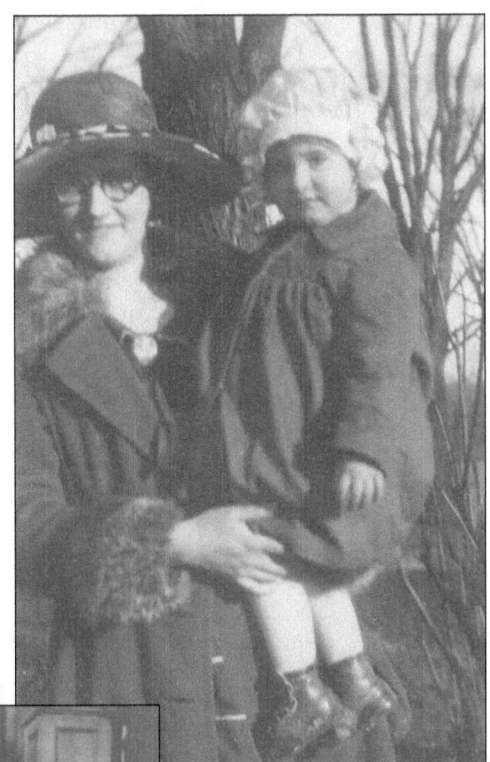

Marcia, Age Two,
with Mother, 1921

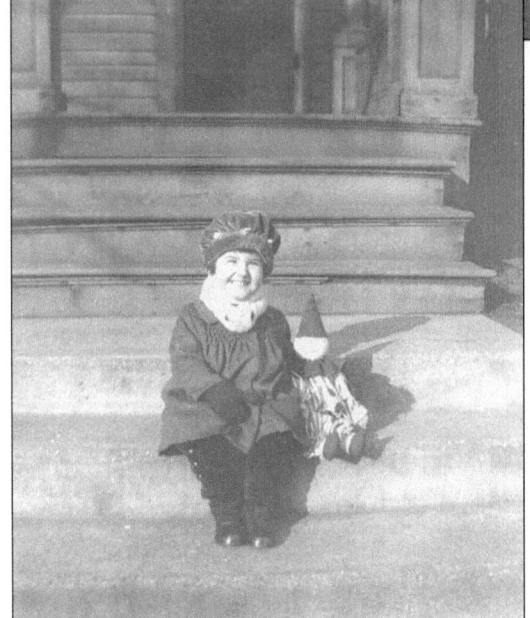

Marcia, Age Three, 1922

"At the same time, I had lots of things to occupy me because I already had a very vivid imagination. I had a toy horse complete with saddle, bridle and stirrups. It was on a frame on four wheels. It was made to sit on and push along. I knew it wasn't a real horse, but he was real to me as we moved along. I imagined I was riding him outside, lots of places. One of the best things about him was a ring in his neck. When you pulled on it, there was a realistic neighing sound. I also had a red pedal car. I was not as interested in the car as I was in the horse. Looking back now, I realize that soon after, when my parents divorced and left, so did my toys. Where did they go? They did not go with me. I don't remember missing them. To me it was the way the adult world worked. Today you were here and had things. Tomorrow there was a new place, new people and unfamiliar things. Perhaps that conditioned me to regard objects as transitory."

She chose not to tell—any of the secrets she was told to keep—about the neighbor man upstairs who had a wooden leg and how he tried to tell her dirty stories and wanted her to sit on his lap—or about the places she went while riding the horse or the friends she saw so clearly—or about the adventures she created. She entertained herself. "They wouldn't have believed me because I was just a child."

And they might have tried to explain to her that the adventures were not real. As if she needed an explanation for the differences between those things she imagined to keep herself entertained and the realities of her parents' secret friends or the sham shooting. As a child she had already reached her conclusions about adults—that they did strange things, expected children to be stupid, were often not so smart themselves, and were not to be trusted. With that knowledge, her newly gained ability to read, and her little suitcase, she entered her grandparents' home.

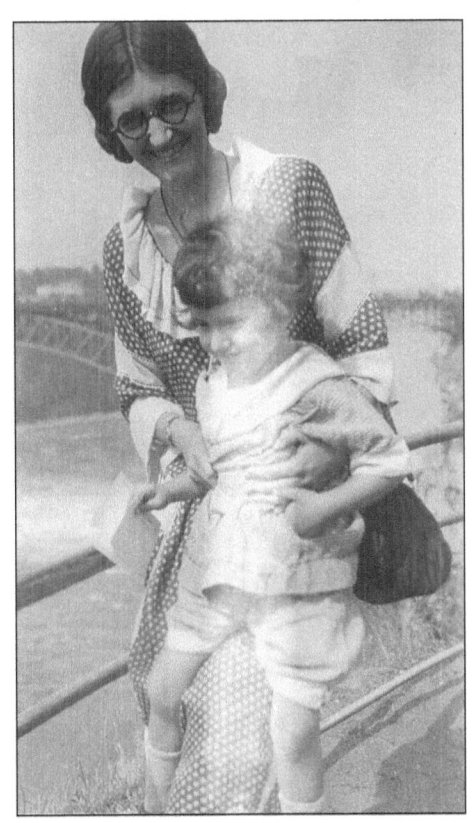

Marcia, Age Four, with Mother, 1923

Orphans Can't Have Two-toned Shoes

> Yet all along a little elf whispers another tale: 'You are different; you're not like anyone in the family; you don't really belong.' There is an unbeliever in the heart.
> It calls the family a fantasy, a fallacy.
> Hillman, J., *The Soul's Code*, p. 64

Marcia's arrival on her grandparents' doorstep in Buffalo may or may not have come as a surprise to her grandmother Adeline Welker. Mrs. Welker, whom Marcia remembers as running the house and running the family, remains a large figure in memories of Marcia's childhood. "She browbeat her poor husband and she couldn't stand any songs about love. She thought love was the most misrepresented thing. She hadn't wanted to get married. I assume it was an arranged marriage."

A photograph in Marcia's collection shows Addie Welker as a young woman with pleasant features, smiling and holding a banjo. A later picture includes her daughter Doris, who is in her twenties or thirties, and a dog. "I don't know when that picture was taken because when I was growing up there were no pets," Marcia commented.

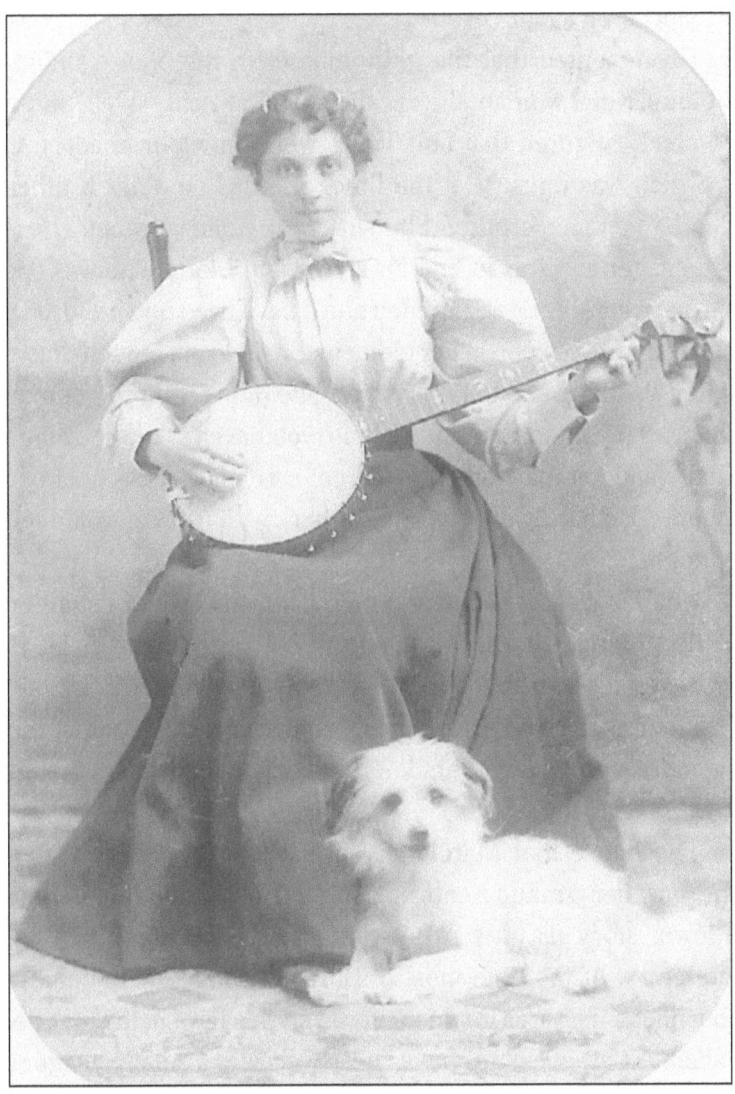

Addie Welker, 1898

In fact, when Marcia was deposited with the Welkers, there were only three in the household, her grandmother, grandfather Charles, and her aunt Doris. "We were not a family. We were a collection of individuals. Out of sight, out of mind. As far as a family was concerned, I didn't exist until I reappeared again."

I commented that the grandmother in the photos didn't look like the imperious woman she recalled. Marcia said, "Well, she was a spoiled child. I figured that out. There were only four children in her family, which was unusual at the time. She had an older brother and sister and a younger brother. She suffered an illness when she was a young teenager and was in bed for a year and I think she was spoiled. She was very independent. I think if she'd have lived one hundred years later she would have been in her element. She told me herself that on the day of her wedding, she told her father she didn't want to get married. 'I've changed my mind.' He said, 'Oh no, you haven't. You're going to go downstairs and get married.' She did not care for marriage. They were not a couple. He hardly ever went anywhere with us. She would tell him to stay home."

Charles Welker had been a merchant who owned a store in Fort Wayne that Marcia recalls when she was a very young child. But in 1923, Mr. Welker sold the store, reportedly unwilling to compete with the chain stores that were developing. Apparently the result of the sale and the store's previous profits left the family comfortable, though not wealthy.

The house that Marcia was brought to by the young couple was the one her grandparents had rented on Humboldt Parkway. It was a lower story flat in a two-flat building. Each home had its own separate entry. At the time most of Buffalo had clearly defined ethnic neighborhoods. The area in which they lived was Jewish; the next nearest was Italian. A Catholic church was nearby as was a small Synagogue. "I went to second and third grades at a school nearby. I soon discovered a classmate who lived on the way to school. She came from a large, jolly

Italian family. Even at my age, I could see that they seemed to enjoy life a lot more than my family did. I invited the little girl to come to play one day. My grandmother was polite but she did question the little girl. Afterward she told me that I shouldn't do that again as 'we don't make friends with them.' I continued to stop at her house occasionally but I never mentioned it at home," Marcia said.

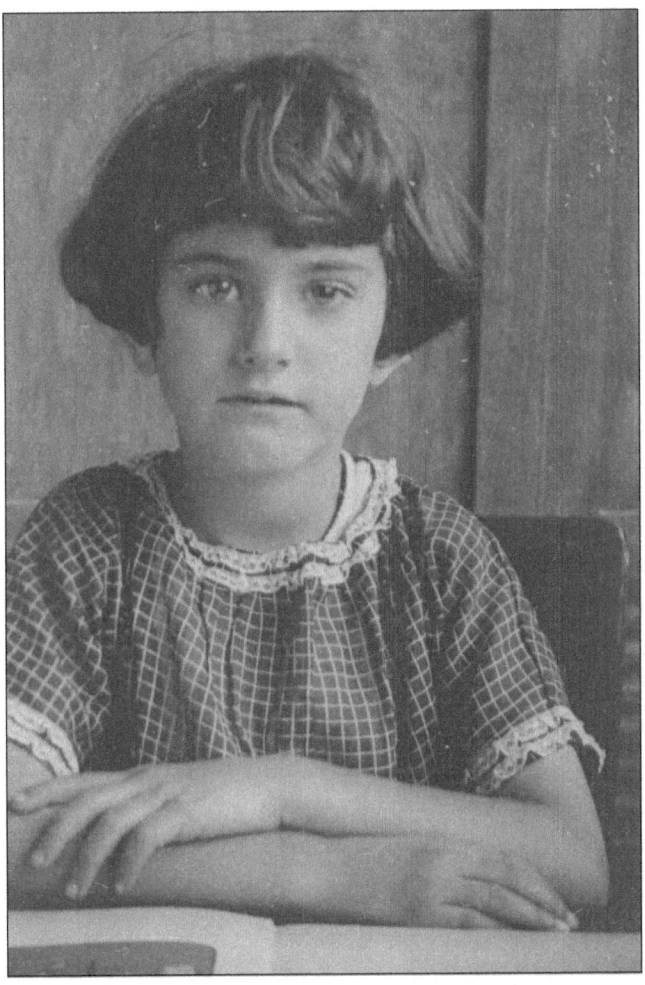

Marcia, 1927

When asked her grandfather's reaction to her arrival on their doorstep, Marcia said, "He didn't say anything. He was there but nobody ever asked him anything. He was there but he wasn't there." Charles Welker and the women in his house continued to live parallel lives, apparently, until his death. "When he died, my grandmother, although not exactly overcome by sorrow, knew enough to be the sorrowing widow. But at home, she laughed and told us that someone had said to her, 'Oh, I thought he had died years ago.' That's when we found out he'd been going around selling some household products for a long time. He spent hours in the homes of people he sold to. The called him 'the old gentleman' and said 'we had the most fun visiting with him—he was so nice.' He had that whole secret life we knew nothing about. He just took the streetcar and would be gone all day. Only when he died did we know what he had been doing," Marcia said.

This man who seemed to have little influence in his family is remembered by his granddaughter as one person who did something just for her, a noteworthy distinction. During the years she lived with them in Buffalo, he took her to the art museum and the zoo on alternate Sundays. Was he aware that he was nurturing a lively imagination, something her *daimon* must have wanted, helping create memories that would influence her painting more than sixty-five years later? Perhaps that recollection contributed to the painting, *The Myr-Lou Zoo*, featured on the cover of her 2004 book *Words and Images*.

Addie Welker's father, Peter Muth, was approximately six years old when his family emigrated from Darmstedt, Germany to the U.S. in 1836. Her mother's family also had emigrated, from Alsace Lorraine. Great-Grandmother Muth, her mother's mother was from a Jewish family. When the family arrived, one of the things they did was to become Presbyterian. The Welker household continued, at least nominally, in that religion. Because of that, and because religion was not really a factor in the household she became a part of, as a child Marcia was unaware of her Jewish heritage. "My family was not particularly observant of anything. They turned against religion. My grandmother went to church, but it was primarily a social occasion, a form of entertainment for her. She came home and discussed what the women wore and how people had behaved. I never saw my grandfather go. I never really understood what was going on.

"My grandfather was a great reader and my grandmother also, but not my aunt. Oh, Auntie would read magazines, but never a book. She was a bright person but she bragged that she never read a book after she left high school. She wasn't intellectually curious. What she thought, I really don't know."

Aunt Doris was just out of high school when the "little orphan" came to live at the house. The fifteen-year difference in their ages may have been part of the reason that she was not fond of the occasional responsibility for the child. Or perhaps she was chafing under her mother's rule. As the "other daughter," the one who hadn't escaped her mother by eloping, she reaped the benefit of added attention. But she also was the focus of her mother's continuing supervision.

"She never really worked. Oh, she did work briefly in an office, just as a fun thing with the girls. She was not prone to housework, liked to stay up late and listen to the radio and get up around eleven in the morning. She went shopping and to the movies a lot. She had a boyfriend and then another friend of his came along and sort of took her over. My grandmother didn't approve, but said she could get engaged. They stayed engaged for eight years!" Asked if she attributed any of her aunt's behavior to her grandmother's influence, Marcia said, "I think so. She (grandmother) was very rigid. Appearances were everything. If you broke your leg in public, you were not to call attention to it. Keep up a front, no matter what. I suppose that in those days, if you got married, you were successful."

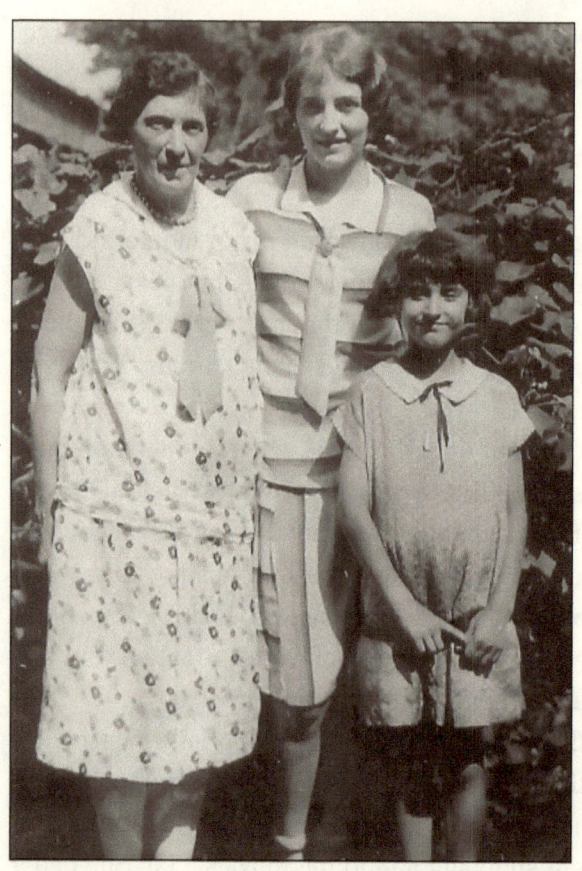

Marcia with Grandmother and Aunt Doris, 1930

As an unintended addition to the Welker household, Marcia occupied a room that housed, among a variety of seldom used items, a glass-fronted bookcase. "The bookcase had doors with a little lock, but the key was in it, so I could get the books. I read from the bottom shelf up as soon as I learned to read. Later, when they knew I could read well, my aunt would choose books she thought were appropriate and mark passages I should read. I don't know if they realized I read everything in the whole book.

"Children back then were to be seen and not heard. If company came, I would be called to come and recite something, but I otherwise was expected to keep to myself. I had things to play with. I had imagination. It was a good childhood."

The play she describes reflects that imagination and something more. Perhaps it's the whimsical perspective that friends and acquaintances consistently use to describe Marcia even now. She had dolls, but she didn't dress them and pretend they were people at a tea party. Instead she undressed them and pretended they were plucked chickens hanging for sale in the farmers' market. Her career choice? Streetcar conductor.

There must have been some classics on those bookshelves because Marcia recalls reading Shakespeare and acting out all the parts. Ariel and Romeo and all the others may have benefited from some of Marcia's excursions into fantasy. Another of her favorites from that period is a book that she still has, a poetry anthology, *Palgrave's Golden Treasury*. Much of the entertainment she manufactured involved characters and activities that only she could see. But she did see them and she did talk to them while she kept to herself, seen and not heard.

As for her vivid fantasies, she didn't mention them to anyone. "I knew they wouldn't believe me or that they would tell me I was wrong. So I just didn't tell them." Too bad for the Welkers. They might have enjoyed hearing about the invented uncle who came regularly to visit her.

"Eidetic, I think that's the word for very vivid images," she said. Although she didn't experience the odors or fragrances of the places she went in her adventures, every other detail, in color, was explicit.

"Because my grandmother often called me the 'poor orphan' I imagined how it would be to live in an orphanage. I recall I wanted some two-tone shoes I'd seen. 'No, orphans can't have two-toned shoes,' Grandmother said. Once she told me that if I didn't do some chore I was to do I could go live in an orphanage. I said, 'Fine, let's go.' I already knew how it would be because I had imagined it all while I was doing the dishes. I was always interested in architecture so I could even see the details of the buildings. The orphanage was one of my favorite places."

Eidetic, according to the dictionary, is indeed the word describing very vivid, but unreal images; characteristic of the imagination of childhood. The word she chose was correct, but Marcia's images and the other world that accompany them have persisted far past childhood, for a lifetime. She closes her eyes and visits the seashore, a restaurant, a market, or any destination she chooses. No one talked her out of her fantastic trips because she kept them to herself.

No one knew she lived with gypsies when she was in the fourth or fifth grade. "I didn't really know any gypsies, but I heard about them and there was a gypsy boy who came to school. I must have read something too. I would come home from school and change my clothes. Then in my mind, I'd go to the gypsy camp and I could see the people in it, what we talked about, everything. It was where I was living. This was something I couldn't tell my family. They thought I was strange enough without that, truthfully."

Her family may have thought she was odd, but not because she was unattached to reality. If anything, her clear awareness of the differences between real and not real seemed strange to them. She attended a play with her grandmother and aunt. That she was dry-eyed and cheery after a sad scene to which others reacted with tears and concern for the heroine prompted a scolding. "Why should I have been upset? It was a play. It wasn't real." Equanimity in one so young must have been disconcerting to Mrs. Welker.

"I realized early on that I had been placed in this family by mistake. I never wanted to do what they wanted me to. Maybe that made me want to succeed at the things they thought were useless—reading and writing. I started writing when I was in the second or third grade, just little things and drawing pictures to illustrate them. But I didn't write about the secret things I imagined. One was real life. The other was my secret."

Sometime around 1929, when Marcia was ten, the Welkers moved back to Fort Wayne. The first house they returned to was the one that the Welkers had lived in before their pursuit of Margaret and Frank Miller had taken them to Buffalo. It was a large two-story house with four or five bedrooms and a basement. A stained glass window about five feet in length decorated an alcove in which a piano was located. The house, on a large lot that had a grape arbor and a small barn in the back, was downtown only a few blocks from the train station. Marcia said, "The government decided to buy the whole block and build the new post office there. Looking back, I'm sure my grandmother and aunt were eager to move to a more fashionable part of town. When the house was torn down they had the stained glass removed and crated. It stayed in the basement at the new house because they never found a place to put it. The new house was in the south part of town on Kinnard Avenue. Although it was smaller, it was a very nice and had a large fenced backyard. Upstairs there was a room that became my room. It had no closets but had eight windows that opened and fastened to the ceiling. The house had been built for a man whose wife had tuberculosis and that room was for her, so that she could get plenty of light and fresh air."

As a child, Marcia was unaware of the fact that the family was more comfortable financially than most others. "The money part later puzzled me. Although there was not any household help when I was a child, I remember my grandmother telling about the help they had years before. She spoke of the Irish girls who learned how to keep house and then got married and left. Looking back, I can see that our standard of living did not change during the Depression. For example, my grandmother and I went East every summer, a day trip by train. We always went Pullman. I remember going to down to the coaches and looking at the "poor people"—my grandmother's explanation. I thought that it looked like they were having a much better time than I was. There were few people in the Pullman and usually my grandmother would strike up a conversation with another lady. She relied on the porter to keep an eye on me as I roamed around the train. Although she would not eat in the dining car or explain why not, she gave me money to have my lunch there.

"At home we had the latest of household gadgets, the best available radio, etc. My grandmother and aunt went to Chicago for a weekend every so often so they could shop at Marshall Field and stay in a hotel. And several times my aunt traveled by train to California to visit a cousin. I didn't realize then how fortunate we were," Marcia said.

As in Buffalo, Grandmother Welker was particular about the friends that Marcia was permitted to have. A few girls from the neighborhood were allowed to come to play. One of those friends that Marcia has kept up with through the years is Gwen Roberts. The Roberts family lived three houses away. That friendship eventually opened the door to events that contributed many scenes to Marcia's store of vivid images.

Scene 4

Books, Cigarettes, and Imagination

As we live we are being invented, though the haphazard events of the day seem to hang on no coherent thread. Childhood makes sense in retrospect.
Hillman, J., *The Soul's Code*, p. 176

Teachers saw something in the girl her family thought of as odd. "School teachers often were extremely kind to me. Most of the time they realized I needed extra work. They encouraged me to read and to write. One teacher I had, when I'd finished what we were required to do, said, 'You go ahead and write something else.' So, I'd write two. Or I'd read extra books. I would say my teachers, all of them through high school and grade school, have been a welcoming influence. Maybe my family would give me books for the holidays, but that was it and you weren't supposed to sit around reading. You were supposed to be doing something useful. Do your chores. And I was so nuts about reading that I used to think my grandmother had eyes in the back of her head.

I'd be dusting till I came to the magazine rack where I would start to read and all of a sudden a voice would say, 'Put that down and get back to dusting.' Or I'd put the garbage out—in those days we wrapped it—and I'd see something I'd missed in the newspaper, the wrapper, and I'd be sitting down reading it.

"Reading books was my life. As I mentioned before, there was a bookcase in my room because I had the room with the leftovers, naturally. I read every one of those books until I reached the top shelf. They were so innocent in some ways to think I wouldn't read. I read everything that came in. I read the two newspapers. I still love newspapers. I can't imagine not reading."

Marcia might have been an even more solitary, sedentary reader and dreamer had it not been for her friend Gwen Roberts. "I was always after her to exercise, to build herself up because she was sort of skinny. Once we built a miniature golf course," Gwen said. She recalled that Marcia was included in many of the Roberts family's activities, along with Gwen's sister Effie and occasionally her older brother.

"They took a vacation at a lake every year for a couple of weeks and they would invite me for part of the time," Marcia said. Gwen recalled taking Marcia along to attend vacation bible school at a Baptist Church. "Mrs. Roberts was English and her husband was Welsh. Gwen was a year older and her sister Effie a year younger than I. We weren't in the same class at school, but close enough to be friends. Her older brother was in high school so we young girls were 'dirt' to him. He ignored us. I loved to go down to their house."

Like Marcia, Gwen didn't think of life at the Welker's house as being cruel for the youngster. Rather, looking back from her 87th year, she characterized the household as strict and straight-laced. Aunt Doris, she mentioned, was "neurotic, always ill." She had no recollection of ever meeting Marcia's father and mentioned that her mother was a nurse at Deaconess Hospital. Apparently she did meet Marcia's mother, Margaret Miller, at some time because she commented, "I didn't care much for her."

The Welker household changed when after eight years of being engaged, Doris' suitor Lee Bernhardt, wrote to say that he had an opportunity to go to China for his work as an engineer. Doris told him to wait; told her mother she was going to Buffalo to visit Margaret; then informed the Welkers by long distance phone call that she and Lee had gotten married. The newlyweds moved to Pennsylvania where Lee took a job as an auto mechanic. They lived in an apartment above the garage and were happy in their new life.

This daughter's elopement was treated differently than Margaret's. Rather than move to Pennsylvania to supervise the young marrieds, Addie Welker managed to bring the couple back to the house in Fort Wayne. Her method was direct and effective. She contacted an acquaintance in management at the local General Electric factory, told him she had a new son-in-law, an engineer, who needed a job. As Marcia tells stories of the events she observed as a young teenager, one can almost imagine Grandmother Welker hanging up the phone after calling the newlyweds to come home, smiling the smile of an achieved manipulator.

Lee's hobbies offered much of interest for Marcia. "He could fly an airplane; he could work on cars; and despite my grandmother's disapproval, his friends would come over on weekends and they would work on cars. He'd let me watch and sometimes ask me to bring a tool or something. And he took a magazine called *Flying Aces* that he let me read."

That magazine was popular in the 1930s among a varied readership because in addition to non-fiction articles about real pilots and their planes, it included instructions for building working models. Even better, there were fictional accounts of aviation-related escapades by dashing heroes. Those tales were deposited in Marcia's vault of varied information, resting beside Shakespeare and items from last week's newspaper.

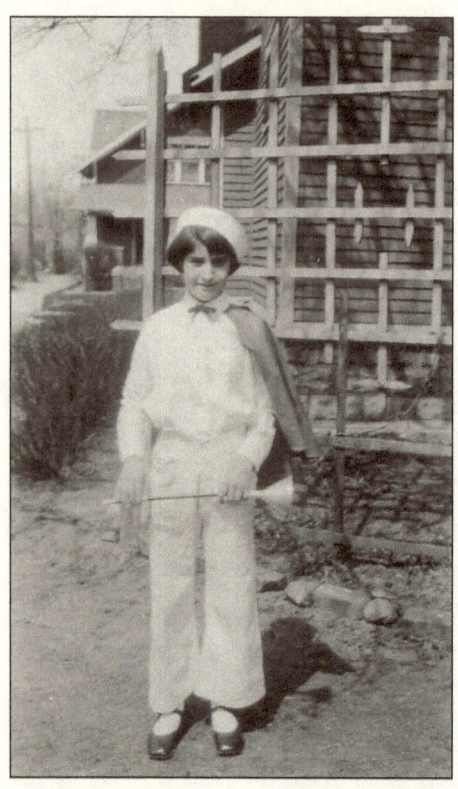

Marcia, Playing a Part in a School Play, 1931

The exploits from the pages of *Flying Aces* probably made one family legend even more vivid. The legend concerned her Uncle Lester, her father's only and older brother. Quoting a one-page account written by Marcia entitled 'Homage to Uncle Lester,' "When the First World War came along, he felt it to be his duty to serve his country but he was basically a pacifist. However, he did join the Army as an aviator but served as an observer not a fighter. After the war, he came back from Europe and became a stunt pilot and a 'wing walker'. His specialty was jumping from one wing of a plane to the other. In 1919 or 1920, he missed his step and fell to his death. Various reasons were given for his lack of concentration on his work and the fact that he had not worn his parachute that day. His mother, who was there, insisted that his mind was not on what he was doing because he had gotten married that day. My other grandmother (Welker) insisted that his death was caused by a plate of radishes he had eaten before going up. Whenever we had a meal with radishes, the sad story of Uncle Lester was retold."

The changes accompanying the addition of Lee to the family may have encouraged a broader sense of adventure in Marcia. Here-and-now activity complemented the tales of fictional characters and of her own cast of invented characters and their lives' details. Besides the weekend afternoon car repair activities in the yard, she and Gwen were interested in the nearby filling station. In the early 1930s, a gas station was a busy and fascinating place, especially for a person with a lively imagination. People stopped at the station for service, not as they do today to self-serve their fuel needs.

Marcia's painting, *A-One Garage*, reflects her memory of an establishment of that sort. This is a beehive of activity. It contains no fewer than twenty people and a dog. Five vehicles are pictured, two of which are in the process of repair. There's also some non-vehicle commerce inside the garage headquarters. There a customer drinks ice cold pop (5 cents says the sign); another eating a candy bar stands at the screen door watching the action outside; two others are completing a transaction at the cash register near a sign advertising a Saturday night dance at the Elk Lodge.

"I learned how to smoke cigarettes at the filling station. An older guy who worked there fixed cars and sold candy. He showed us how to smoke. When Gwen and I learned to smoke, we couldn't afford cigarettes. If we had some, we'd crawl out her bedroom window and sit on the roof to smoke. She probably wouldn't want to remember that now. I think that other, older people may have learned other things at the filling station," Marcia said. I think I caught a twinkle of amusement as she recalled those escapades.

Lee Bernhardt, apparently adapting to life in the Welker house, became a valued G.E. employee and a dutiful member of Addie Welker's family group. "Lee traded his Lincoln Roadster for a Buick so we could all ride. He became the driver for the family." Accepting Addie Welker's will? That seems likely. Marcia said, "My aunt told me that the reason they had no children was that Grandmother told them there were to be no children. She told me their relationship was like brother and sister. You can see why—Grandmother wouldn't allow any doors in the house to be shut, ever."

Perhaps Marcia (and her *daimon*?) would have adapted also, progressing from teen-aged "orphan" to suitable young womanhood. Perhaps she would have continued through high school thriving on the attention of teachers, dusting, reading everything available to her and visiting the gypsy camp. But, Gwen Roberts and her family were at least partly responsible for an important change that made Marcia's fifteenth year memorable.

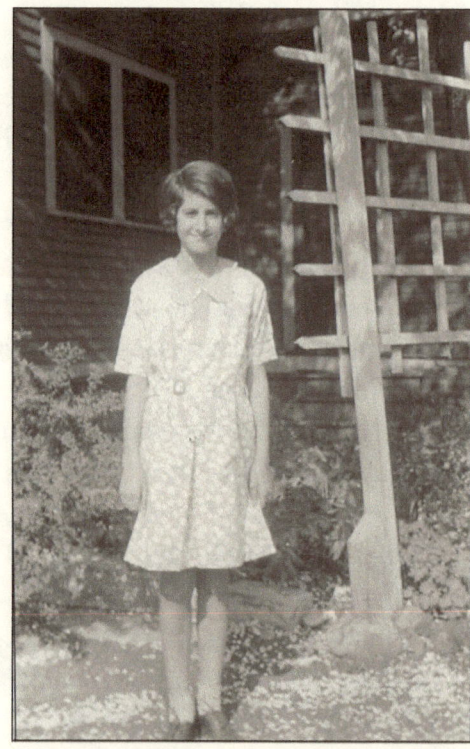

Marcia, Age 12, 1931

A Ticket To A More Interesting Life

The acorn seems to follow just this sort of limited
pattern. It does not indulge in long-term philosophies.
It disturbs the heart, it bursts out in a temper . . . .
It excites, calls, demands—but rarely does it offer a
grand purpose. Hillman, J., *The Soul's Code*, p. 197

"The neighbors talked about Gwen's mother. They would say, 'Tsk, she's not in there cleaning. She's on the porch reading.' And sometimes she bought baked goods, didn't bake her own! I thought it was wonderful. She was complicit in my leaving home to live with my father." Perhaps Marcia's *diamon* was complicit as well. Perhaps it "excited, called, demanded—didn't engage in long term philosophies"—just as Hillman describes. The pleasant afternoons on the Roberts' porch paled before the prospect of a move to North Tonawanda. "My father sent for me because he thought I should have a more interesting life," Marcia said.

"I had told him about Gwen and her family. We arranged that he would send Mrs. Roberts a bus ticket and instructions for me," Marcia said. Recalling the opinions of her father and Mrs. Roberts and others about her decision to leave the Welkers in Fort Wayne, she said, "The thought was that my grandmother didn't do anything much and my aunt was a lazy hypochondriac and my grandfather disappeared every day." Gwen's mother apparently agreed. Gwen still recalls going to the bus station to see Marcia off. The two good friends corresponded regularly after Marcia's secret departure. We can only imagine the thoughts the teenagers shared in those letters.

"Out of sight, out of mind." Marcia used that phrase to describe her family's way of relating to one another. She didn't tell them she was leaving; she just got on the bus. When she arrived, her father sent the Welkers a telegram to let them know she had arrived to stay. No one demanded that she return to Fort Wayne. She was out of sight. After nearly ten years at her rather stolid grandparents' home, the orphan was off on an adventure.

Marcia joined her father and his wife Olga in North Tonawanda, outside Buffalo, in their apartment. She became an employee of her father's drugstore, Lester Drug. Naming the store Lester was her father's way of acknowledging his brother's help in launching his career as a pharmacist. Before he entered pharmacy school, he lacked tuition money. Lester, the wing-walker ensconced in family lore for his pre-death meal of radishes, visited Frank in a dream each night for a week. In the dream, Lester provided the numbers of horses in specific races. Frank placed each bet as "instructed" and those horses were all winners. The tuition problem was solved. And that was the last her father saw of his brother. Frank Miller told that story for the truth, and true or not, it's still a great story. Lester Drug was a lasting tribute to the source of those ethereal instructions.

Marcia's 2002 painting *Fourth of July Parade* allows a peek at a version of Lester Drug. She included a series of storefronts as background for the parade. The business in the center is Lester Drug. It stands between the First National Bank and a discount furniture store. The drugstore window signs advertise ice cream, tobacco, perfume, soda fountain, candy and cigars as notable wares. Coty face powder is on sale.

Marcia's life did become far more interesting in New York than in Indiana. She described her new environment, "There were two towns, Tonawanda and North Tonawanda. As I recall it they were divided by a canal or a river. We had the only drugstore in the area so we were a busy place. North Tonawanda opened up a whole new way of life for me. I did have to spend a large portion of my time helping at the store, but I also had time to roam around town and its outskirts. I was particularly fond of being near the water. In one place there was a bridge with a small building in the center where the bridge-keeper stayed. When a ship or big boat came along, he would swing the bridge around so that it was no longer aligned horizontally and the ship could pass. I made friends with the keeper and if I was there when bridge had to be moved he would let me stay on. I was also friends with a classmate whose family owned a small café that they lived just behind. The living quarters were divided from the business only by a heavy curtain. I recall them being Polish. We lived in a small apartment about a block from the drugstore."

She worked in the drugstore, entered high school and spent her free afternoons with Olga's mother. Mrs. Goldstein, originally from Hungary, kept an Orthodox Jewish home. Although her father and Olga were not observant of all the religious traditions, Marcia was an observer of all around her. Many times she would go with Mrs. Goldstein to the Reform Synagogue to attend Friday service or sit with her while she lit the Shabbat candles. They also celebrated Passover. But she did not actually embrace her heritage until much later in life. In fact, she'd never been aware of that background because her grandmother had attended Presbyterian Church services on those occasions when they did participate. She does recall, however, that once her grandmother had remarked to her that she looked Jewish. She gave it little thought at the time.

At fifteen, thoughts of her family background interested Marcia far less than the more immediate activities at the store. For example, before her arrival there, all she knew about sex she had learned from books. During her first weeks at the drugstore, her father "explained things." Her observer's eye must have been sharpened after he further explained how customers would behave when they came to buy condoms. He said that if men intended to buy "rubbers" (not on public display in the 1930s) they would ask to see the druggist. But rather than speak to him about intimate items, women purchasing sanitary napkins would ask for her help. So the fifteen year-old with her new worldly understanding would lead them to the back of the store, a suitable spot for such items.

Marcia also accepted her father's tutelage in following the Miller family tradition of acting. But the role she acquired did not put her on a formal stage. Rather, she acted as a shill. This opportunity resulted from another of Mr. Miller's enterprises. In a separate building about a block from the drugstore, he installed pinball machines to attract youngsters and to encourage them to part with their spare change. Marcia enticed her age-mates to play by demonstrating the joy of inserting coins and flipping paddles. Certainly it was a far cry from her solitary Shakespearean performances, but surely entertaining because she played for free using slugs instead of money. The police shut that business down before two weeks passed.

Discovering new talents and interests in this new environment could only consume a part of the teen-age Marcia's attention. School must be considered. In order to enroll in high school, she needed a birth certificate. The request for Doris Miller's document came back NONE. Then her father recalled that her mother had named her Marcia. The official document she received produced another surprise. Her actual legal name was different than she'd thought. Addie Welker had called her by the name Doris, the same name as her aunt. Marcia had believed that was her name. Yet the birth certificate declared "Marcia Miller." So, along with a new school and new surroundings, she had a new name to adapt to. Her *daimon* must have been delighted.

Many years later, she chose to add the name Muth, her grandmother's family name, as her middle name. Although she never changed her name legally, she subsequently chose to use Marcia Muth as her professional name.

Frank Miller may have had a strictly paternal interest in Marcia's development, hoping to provide her a more interesting life. He may also have correctly assessed that the bright young woman could be very useful as a part of the Lester Drug work force. Did he consider the possibility that she also could be a source of discord in his marriage? Or did he only recall his young confederate in those "we don't need to mention this" excursions they had made without her mother?

Had he discussed the decision with Olga prior to purchasing the bus ticket that brought Marcia to New York? No journals or diaries are available that record the actions or thoughts of any of the members of the newly-created family group. But it is safe to assume that adjustments were required of all of them. Marcia and Frank had the benefit of prior experience with one another. Frank had, briefly, played the role of on-site father to this child before. Marcia skillfully had managed her existence in her grandparents' Fort Wayne household. But Olga, only twelve years older than Marcia, was relatively new as a parent and had never shared her husband's attention with a teen-aged daughter. Certainly if any degree of harmony were to be achieved in the apartment, all present would need to "hum the same tune."

Scene 6

Learning About Life—At the Drugstore

> Though this accompanying image shadowing your life is the bearer of fate and fortune, it is not a moral instructor or to be confused with conscience."
> Hillman, J., *The Soul's Code*, p. 9

Quick learner that she was, Marcia aptly accomplished an assortment of tasks at the drugstore. But, at least once she seemed less than competent at her assignment. She was to cook a batch of chocolate syrup for the store's soda fountain. The basement location of the stove was not her favorite place. She had not abandoned her love of reading in favor of her "more interesting life." Instead, she sometimes combined reading with less challenging chores. The chocolate-stirring qualified as less challenging. So, she began reading. Transported by literature, she ignored the syrup until she smelled the pot scorching. Frank did not punish her, but did point out the cost of ruining a batch of syrup.

Jobs that were more interesting received her full attention. A favorite was making deliveries. The neighborhood was home to a Catholic convent. As the "delivery girl," she had to step lively because she walked rather than bicycled on those deliveries. Frank had vetoed her request for a two-wheeler. The nuns' delivery request required particular speed because their frequent Sunday afternoon purchase was ice cream. The good sisters usually tipped her, adding a further incentive to the opportunity to observe the scenes of the streets. It seems they also lodged in her store of memories.

The book *A World Set Apart, Memory Paintings* (2007) includes a reproduction of Marcia's 2005 painting of nine nuns, apparently on the way to prayers. One carries a prayer book, six hold glowing candles and the last carries a single red rose. No other figures join the group. The gray stone wall that forms the background is broken only by the wood-framed door they will enter. Vivid green grass carpets their way. The starkness evokes the nuns' way of living their faith. The artist's notes state, "In the thirties you often saw nuns dressed in their distinctive habits. No matter what your religious affiliation, you always felt a sense of respect toward them. Also sometimes a sense of awe for they were women who had given up their private lives to serve the public good. It was the nuns who were the driving force in the schools, the clinics, orphanages and old age homes."

The painting's simplicity is striking for its difference from most other Muth memory paintings. Those others are packed with people, activity and details. The nuns' faces are not even visible, adding further simplicity. She displays that same simplicity in a drawing entitled *Nuns Walking* that accompanies a poem "The Nuns" in her book *Words and Images* (2004):

> I saw the nuns walking
> Close at hand
> In one straight line

Single file
Clothed in black and white
Like a photo
From a much earlier time
Now simply
Buried in memory's scrapbook

Another favorite delivery destination for the young adventurer was the "red light district." The working girls fascinated her with their chatty friendliness. Also enticing were their ten cent tips, a large sum for her effort. On one delivery to the area she missed what would certainly have been another exciting experience. She was spared a ride in a paddy wagon when one of the policemen conducting a raid recognized her. "Let her be, she's only the kid from the drugstore," he said.

An essay contest in English class provided an opportunity to share some of her experiences. She and a friend apparently pushed the limits of North Tonawanda sensibilities with their choices of topics. Her friend wrote on the topic of "the pleasures of taking a bath." Marcia topped her with her exposition entitled "Night and Day in the Red Light District." Neither was considered suitable for the contest nor for reading aloud to the class. "That was my first intimation of the power of censorship," she said.

Among her drugstore duties, Marcia also assisted her father in a mail order business. Frank Miller sold "yo-ho pills" by mail. Advertised in cheap pulp magazines, the pills purported to "improve male vigor." Marcia packaged and mailed the batches. The price was one dollar.

Another of Frank's enterprises also involved Marcia. He sold liquor on the side. Her job was to place counterfeit tax stickers on the bottles. She's still not certain of where the liquor actually came from, but it obviously didn't pass through the regular route from wholesale to retail.

Addie Welker's domain back in Fort Wayne offered none of the exciting opportunities Marcia encountered in North Tonawanda. The facts of life, nuns, Jewish religious rituals, censorship, police raids, the red light district, mail order commerce and bootleg liquor brought Marcia new understanding of the world and much to store for later use.

Olga Thinks It's Not Working Out

Fathers have been far away for centuries . . . .
Hillman, J., *The Soul's Code*, p. 81

In 1936, Adolph Hitler was Chancellor of Germany. Nazi incursions into regions adjacent to Germany had begun. Jews in Germany were threatened with arrest if they voted. In the United States, President Franklin Roosevelt's New Deal made slow progress toward restoring the nation's economy. Wages were low—the national average annual salary that year was $1,600. Bread was eight cents per loaf and milk 48 cents per gallon. Those prices that seem so low today were beyond the means of many. Unemployment was still a problem for the country in 1936.

Although the country's general economy lagged that year, Frank Miller's abilities as an entrepreneur had set the scene for him to take a step up. He began negotiations to open a new drugstore. He planned to move the family to nearby Kenmore, New York to locate near the new business. The new store was in downtown Buffalo.

The move took place in the middle of the school year. Following the move, Marcia enrolled in high school in Kenmore, but she wasn't happy there. She missed her friends in North Tonawanda.

Marcia doesn't recall that she had any major conflicts with her stepmother, Olga, during the time she lived with Frank and her. But, there may have been problems in the marriage that Marcia was not the source of. "My father said one time that he had a theory. That was that he would only spend seven years with any one woman. He had been married to someone between my mother and Olga and that only lasted a few years. They married not long after he and my mother divorced. They had one child, the only other child my father had. She was born ten years after I was. I found out later that even though he and Olga did stay married, he kept a mistress after the first few years of their marriage. It was Olga's sister," Marcia said.

Maybe the teen-aged Marcia balked only because she hoped to be allowed to stay in school at North Tonawanda when the move occurred. Or perhaps she had no clear notion of what she hoped to accomplish by her resistance to the changes. Adolescents often don't have.

As soon as the school year was over, Frank Miller had a talk with Marcia that made clear to her that her situation was about to change again. Marcia recalled the explanation. "He said, 'Olga thinks it's no longer useful for you to be here.' I realize now that I wasn't needed to work at the store any longer and there was no good reason for me to be there. What he said implied that Olga made the decision. But evidently he didn't disagree. Anyway, I had no choice but to leave.

"I really didn't know what to do," she said.

The only logical choice then was for Marcia to pack her suitcase and her Gorky novels and return to Fort Wayne.

She was allowed to return to her grandparents' house for the rest of the summer. They soon decided that it was time for her parents to take some responsibility. So her grandmother took her back to Buffalo at the end of the summer.

As Marcia tells her recollection of the events when she was returned to Buffalo, one can imagine her being the sixteen year old equivalent of a hot potato. She was figuratively tossed from hand to hand among Margaret, Frank and her grandmother. Her mother had married a younger man and had not told him that she had a teen-aged daughter. She refused to do anything about or for Marcia. Frank also said he couldn't do anything. Then her grandmother declared that she too would no longer be involved. Frank decided to hand the problem to the Children's Aid Society. Marcia became a ward of the State.

Learning About "The People"— And The Streets

Because we walk about in fields of psychic realities that influence our lives, we have to broaden the notion of environment in terms of "deep ecology," the hypothesis that the planet is a living, breathing, and self-regulating organism.

Since anything around can nourish our souls by feeding imagination, there is soul stuff out there. Hillman, J., *The Soul's Code*, p. 153

"We have our standards," the proprietor said, "only one man in a room at a time." Marcia had returned to Buffalo after a brief summer's stay in Fort Wayne. Her first residence was the local YWCA. The Children's Aid Society persuaded her father to pay the rent for her. After nearly a year there, he stopped paying. So, she took a light-housekeeping room in the establishment with the "standards." Before long she understood the reason for the proprietor's stipulation. At least one of the other tenants was a prostitute, unable to work due to having a case of syphilis.

Marcia's new accommodation was an L-shaped room that contained a bed, a chair, a card table, a bureau with a mirror, a two-plate burner and a gas heater. All that for $3.00 per week. The three floor building housed eight tenants on each of the upper two floors and there were three or four apartments on the first level. Marcia and the seven other occupants on the third floor shared one bathroom. "Soul stuff" indeed.

"I remember a woman, a clerk at a nearby grocery store, who once gave me an apple. It was very touching because she had no reason to do that." A salesman on her floor used each weekend to achieve drunkenness. Even though the circumstance was not exactly homey, Marcia felt welcome there. "Everyone there helped each other. Lots of people were having a hard time in those years."

Money was scarce for many people. The youngster managed to reduce her expenses by eating only one meal a day. Instead of lunch, she visited the art museum at midday. She became a regular dinner patron at a diner that had a daily special for twenty-five cents a meal. "I recall feeling resentful of people that I saw going into a nice restaurant to eat, where they might pay a dollar for a meal. I could only go to the twenty-five cent place. So, I can understand how people feel when they have nothing. It showed me the value of education and that was part of what convinced me that I would go to college."

Details of the site of those daily specials were fixed in her memory. Diners later became a frequent subject of her memory paintings. *Al's Diner* is the subject of a 1995 painting included in *A World Set Apart*. The calendar on Al's wall shows August 1938. Ellis Dairy sponsored the calendar. The scene includes nine diners and three waitresses plus the star of the show, the cook. The clock on the wall indicates 12:25, so this is a lunch crowd. Top price on the menu is twenty cents for which one receives two eggs, bacon, potatoes and toast. A hamburger is only ten cents. Details such as those tempt a viewer to study the painting closely. One who does is rewarded by finding a copy of *Movie News* on a back counter, apparently available to a waitress for reading during slack time.

In 1996, she painted *Jody's Diner*. This is a breakfast scene in a smaller diner, one that has only the counter, no booths. In 2006, Marcia revisited a diner in the painting *Lunch Counter*. The cook, sporting a t-shirt labeled ED'S DINER, smokes a cigarette while tending the grill. Marcia's perspective in this painting is different from the other two diner paintings. The view is from behind and above the grill. The result is that the faces of the diners are visible as are the details of the scene behind the counter. She explained in the text of *A World Set Apart* that while the scenes and the details in her paintings are combinations of memories, some current material is added to the minute details. "I borrow the names of family and friends including birthdates, telephone numbers and street addresses. Sometimes I use the date of the day I am painting. And whenever I can, I use my birth year, nineteen nineteen."

Back in 1936, she was busy making the memories she would paint many decades later. A minor living alone without parental supervision acquired a new status. Marcia was now a ward of the State—little different from being an orphan, but without the imaginary orphanage she'd visited while living in Fort Wayne. The status did have an advantage because the National Youth Administration assisted its charges to find employment. She received an assignment to a part-time filing job at a small cancer research hospital. The pay was $6.50 per week. She made do with that because she received no money from either her parents or her grandparents.

The unchallenging work and short hours did not distress Marcia. Other matters occupied her active mind. She continued to read widely. In particular, Maxim Gorky's novels depicting heroic qualities in the struggles of the daily lives of the "people" touched her imagination. "When I left (her father's and Olga's apartment) I was carrying my Gorky novel," she recalled. Although she didn't limit her reading to Russian novels, something in Gorky's work affected her. Gorky's

Marxist political stance reflected his personal experience and his deep distress at the inhumanity of society's treatment of those considered the lowest. His writing succeeded less in politicizing the young Marcia than in arousing her curiosity about all types of people, particularly the down-on-their-luck type of people of whom Gorky wrote.

She didn't mention whether she knew the details of the life of Aleksey Maksimovich Peshkov, who had chosen the name Maxim Gorky. But, an interesting parallel was there if she found it. He also was raised by his maternal grandparents. In his case, childhood from age eight was marked by often cruel conditions as an apprentice and as a dishwasher on a Volga steamer. Those days could not have been called "a good childhood" as Marcia had characterized hers.

In addition to time for reading, Marcia's freedom gave her a new opportunity her *daimon* must have loved. She said, "The streets were safe then, not like now." She set out to learn about life by traveling the streets. She intended to learn about "the people." A youthful romanticism or her *daimon* urging her on; whatever the various stimuli, Marcia spent hours walking the streets of Buffalo, talking with those she met and taking it all in.

During work hours, Marcia wore a dress. But for roving, she chose slacks and a shirt with a tie. Given her slight stature, she could have easily been mistaken for a young boy. Everything was a potential source of new information, for understanding more about life and "the people." Some of those people approached her with various propositions. She said, "Sure, some people would approach me and say, 'hey, would you like to hmhmmm(sic)?' I'd say 'no, I'm not interested' and they'd say 'okay' and leave me alone. One time a man offered me a hundred dollars. He said he didn't want to do anything with me himself, just wanted to watch me with another girl. 'No, not interested,' I said. Actually, sex has never been of particular interest to me, ever."

Other interesting characters she met were Communists holding forth on street corners. They offered passersby pamphlets or invitations to lectures where free food was served. "Their ideology didn't put me off, but their lack of cleanliness did. And some of them tended to try to look down my blouse while talking with me. So, I cut short my flirtation with Communism," she said. "I also attended a religious revival once because they served refreshments."

Living alone, even among kind co-tenants at the rooming house, did create a degree of vulnerability for Marcia. Once she had a serious illness, probably pneumonia, which lingered for two weeks or more. During that time, she essentially had to fend for herself entirely. She does recall she woke one day and saw her father and Olga in her room. They didn't say anything but did leave her a bag of oranges. "Someone must have informed him I was sick," she said. Her description of that illness and later frequent chest problems and subsequent medical advice to live in a dry climate suggest that she has had a lifelong problem with asthma and/or chronic bronchitis. Treatment for such illnesses in the 1930s was mainly rest, but doing so alone may have encouraged her developing an attitude that she said she's long held, "A person can be a victim or a survivor. I am not a victim."

Her Fort Wayne relatives never visited her when she was living at the rooming house. Her mother, also living in Buffalo, did visit on a few occasions. She usually brought some packaged exotic foods and a carton of cigarettes. Marcia appreciated the foods, not because she enjoyed them but because she could use them to barter with acquaintances for foods she actually liked. Margaret Miller Newland had many concerns to occupy her—her teaching of psychiatric nursing and her young husband Fred among them. She was probably pleased that Marcia was handling life on her own and therefore did not attempt to direct her. "On a few occasions I was invited to my mother's apartment for lunch. But she asked me never to say I was her daughter if anyone came while I was there. My mother did comment one time that she thought I would probably turn out to be an interesting person," Marcia said.

"My mother was given to unusual gestures. Once she gave me

a dollar and said, 'I want you to take this and spend it all on dinner.' So I went and had a meal that had five courses. After two or three courses, they brought some sherbet. I said, 'No, I'm not ready for dessert. I'll have the rest of my meal.' I didn't know about cleansing the palate. I just wanted to be sure to get the rest of that meal," she said. More education in the ways of the world!

Marcia decided that it was time to return to formal education, although she had learned much in her time "among the people." The necessary first step was to complete high school. But the regular high school was no longer a fit for the night-time explorer. In many ways she was advanced beyond her age. She enrolled at the Hutchinson Central Evening School, a night school that primarily enrolled immigrants, and received her diploma after two years. Attending McGill University in Canada became her goal as she completed high school with excellent grades. But, she hadn't the money that dream required.

Still, she and her *daimon* were ready for different circumstances. Events in the world that year, 1939, particularly the beginning of war in Europe concerned her. Certainly changes were in the air. Marcia looked toward her future. She'd not formulated any particular long-range plan to replace her dream of McGill University. But she did take a next step. The soon-to-be-twenty year-old night school graduate contacted her grandmother Welker to ask if she could return to live in their house in Fort Wayne.

You Can Stay If...

The more my life is accounted for by what already occurred in my chromosomes, by what my parents did or didn't do, and by my early years now long past, the more my biography is the story of a victim.
Hillman, J., *The Soul's Code*, p. 6

"You can live here without paying room and board," Addie Welker said, "but you will have to have a job." With that statement, she declared the rules for Marcia's return to Fort Wayne in 1939. At twenty years old, equipped with her high school diploma and a broader view of life, Marcia moved back into the house.

At least one family member took note of the differences between the girl who had left and the young woman who returned. Lee Bernhardt wanted to enlist her in his campaign to keep women drivers off American highways. He tried to get her to sign a pledge that she would never drive. "It was sad in a way. I had thought he was great when I was a kid, but he didn't approve of me anymore. Oh, he was always nice, but, he didn't think women should go to college and he didn't approve of people who wrote poetry." She was not suitable on at least two counts. The man who had been at least neutral in regard to her interests now seemed to have joined the ranks of Addie's effort to make Marcia fit into the prescribed mode.

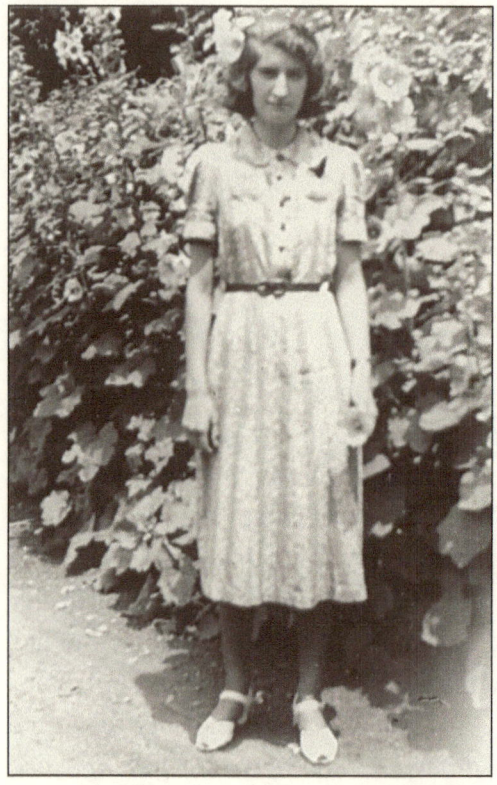

Marcia, 1939

The job that she found offered thirteen dollars per week. She worked in the stock room at a Murphy's variety store. Her grandparents approved of that endeavor even though it was seasonal work—not a permanent solution. Although she had met her grandmother's stipulation that a job was the first priority, Marcia had a personal priority also. She planned to begin taking college courses. No family member actively sought to dissuade her. In fact, she recalls that during a visit to Fort Wayne her mother commented, "Oh, let her go ahead. I'll be the first to congratulate her if she finishes." That was the extent of the support she received. "My mother had gone to school and had a degree, so I wondered why they felt I wasn't supposed to have any help to go. I've thought since that if I hadn't been a strong person, I would have thought there was something wrong with me," she said.

She followed her grandmother's advice that she enroll in a shorthand and typing course that first semester. "After one class session, I switched to English Literature." *Daimon* at work?

Sometime that first semester, she had an opportunity for a permanent job. She could have been assistant manager at a small five and dime store. "Take it," the family said, "you can go places." The five and dime stores became a memory that later appeared in her 1992 painting *Dime Store*. The bustling store in the painting includes a lunch counter and several separate counters displaying items ranging from pots and pans to socks and ties. Although it was an interesting place, and apparently she was seen as having potential for advancement, Marcia did not consider retail as a long-term career choice.

A chance encounter in English Literature class opened a new route for her. "I happened to sit next to a girl and I told her my family's name. 'Oh,' she said, 'my grandfather is a friend of theirs so I know who you are. I just got a job at the public library. They're hiring. Why don't you go down and try?'

"I did, the next day, and got hired, not because I was a reader, though that would have been logical, but because the man hiring knew my grandmother. He thought I could be a typist. I didn't tell him otherwise. I couldn't type at all.

"I thought it would be a good job, even though I couldn't type and I thought it was better than being assistant manager at the dime store. But my family didn't agree. They said I'd do better in retail. 'But I don't want it. I like this,' I said. And my grandfather asked, 'You mean they're going to pay you to hand out books?' I decided to keep the job."

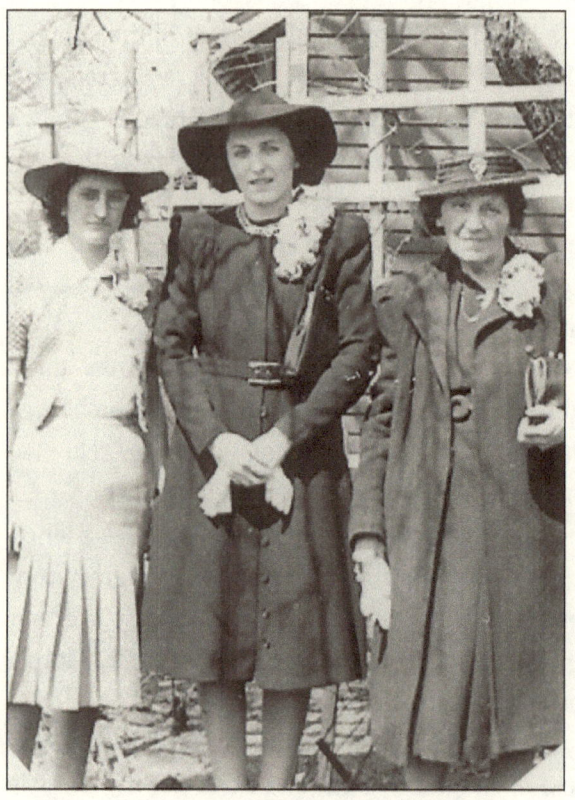

Marcia, Aunt Doris, Grandmother, 1940

The new library employee chose clothing that suited her job. She wore a jumper with large pockets and a white blouse. For a time, Marcia's jumper pockets served a special purpose. They stored the cataloging cards containing her typing errors. Her subterfuge succeeded, but only for a while. Perhaps someone noticed a sudden shortage of blank cards.

Her supervisor realized that her skills would be better used in other library duties—not requiring typing. Her intelligence, her interest in learning and her fascination with books served her well. The library director encouraged her to enroll in a certification course designed to prepare librarians to meet standards in a new Indiana law. The one month course administered by the American Library Association was held in Indianapolis at the Public Library. Completing the course and one additional year's experience would fully qualify her as a public librarian.

The fact that full time college study was beyond her financial grasp made the course an attractive option. She never dreamed of working only until she could get married, as her grandmother and aunt would have hoped. And respectable career choices for women were limited in those days, particularly any that required college education. Women were steered toward becoming teachers, nurses, secretaries, or librarians. Or, there was always retail sales. Taking the librarian certification course seemed a logical choice.

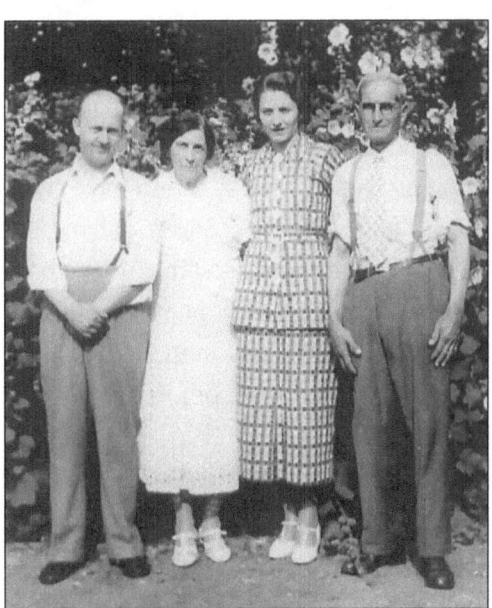

Fred Newland, Addie Welker, Doris Bernhardt, Charles Welker, 1940

During the period after she returned to Fort Wayne, two events occurred that emphasized for Marcia a question for which she has never found a clear answer. The first related to a speech problem that she'd had since childhood. In those days, it was called "tongue tied." In that situation the tongue is attached too firmly by the frenum to the lower structure of the jaw. This results in the growing child's having difficulty enunciating word sounds that require upward movement of the tongue. Remedy is a simple clipping of the frenum to free the movement of the tongue. "Lisping was cute when I was young, but it's not so cute when you get to be older. The 'l' words were always a problem and 'br.' So, when I was back with the family I said I wanted to have that repaired. They said, 'Fine, but that's not our responsibility. If you want it done, you pay for it.' Even then I knew I wanted to be able to speak in front of groups and I didn't want to be hampered.

"I went to a doctor and he told me that it could be done although it wouldn't be exactly as if it had been done when I was a child. After I had it done, I had several sessions with a speech therapist. And that pretty much took care of the lisping except if I got excited and forgot. And I did pay for it."

The second event that caused Marcia's question also involved medical care, in particular, payment for care she needed. "The same thing happened when I had to have an appendectomy. The bill was fifty dollars for the surgeon, sixty dollars for a week in the hospital and ten dollars for the anesthetist that was to be given to him in a plain envelope. The grandparents told me it was my obligation to pay for it all. I didn't have it, so I called my mother to ask her for the money. Her response was, 'Don't they have some kind of welfare in that state?' I paid it out in installments.

"I don't have any malice toward them about those things; I just never understood how they were about money," Marcia said.

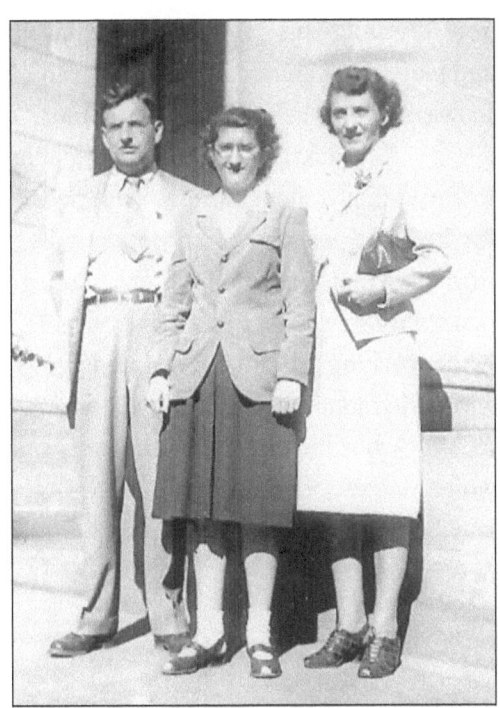

Lee Bernhardt, Marcia, Doris
Bernhardt, 1941

Work and school occupied her as the country moved nearer to entering World War II. Beginning in 1941, after Pearl Harbor, almost everyone in the United States reconsidered everything, with a view to doing their patriotic duty. Marcia thought she might contribute by becoming a nurse. Failing the entrance physical, probably due to her weak lungs, ended that possibility. Instead, she chose to continue becoming a librarian and to plant a Victory Garden.

Also on the home front, Lee Bernhardt attempted to enlist in the Navy. His supervisor at the General Electric factory intervened, explaining that he was essential in his job. He was assigned to duties that frequently required travel to Boston. "My aunt found out he was seeing some one there. She told me, but not much about it. He wanted to leave. But he never left. He paid me to buy a record about love—'I Can't Give

You Anything But Love' or something. He paid me to buy that record and play it. My aunt paid me a dollar to break it with a hammer. So I did. I always felt sorry for him. He got more and more withdrawn."

After completing the certification requirements, Marcia took a job in a small college library. That new certificate opened another door for her. She learned of an opportunity at the University of Michigan through which she could achieve a college degree in library science. The possibility was doubly attractive because she could take college courses while working full-time. It seemed perfect for a studious young woman with little money and a strong will to achieve. "I remember going by bus to Ann Arbor for the interview. I was wearing a demure plaid skirt and white blouse and ner-vously clutching my new librarian's cre-dentials," she said.

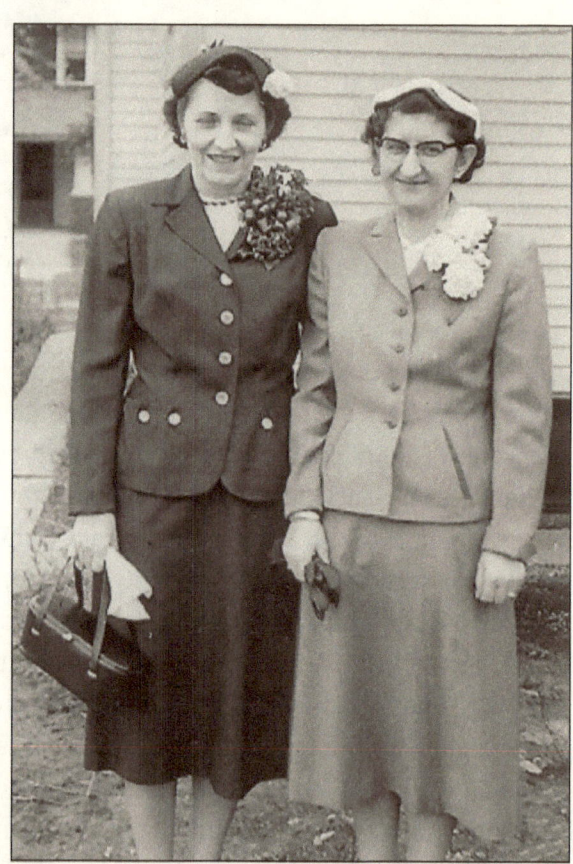

Doris Bernhardt and Marcia, 1943

You Can Go But...

All of a sudden and out of nowhere a child shows who she is and what he must do.
Hillman, J., *The Soul's Code*, p. 13

Being hired by the University of Michigan was the 1943 equivalent of the bus ticket that took Marcia to her father in North Tonawanda.

She broke the news to her family. Aunt Doris thought she should stay in Fort Wayne. Grandmother Welker's main comment was another ultimatum. The previous, "You can stay but you must have a job," was now overshadowed by "If you leave, you'll never get a penny of my money." The melodramatic tone of that edict held little weight with Marcia. She had no notion that there was any money from her grandmother on the horizon anyway. "I thought I'd achieved my life's goal," she said, remembering her excitement at the prospect of all that the university could mean to her.

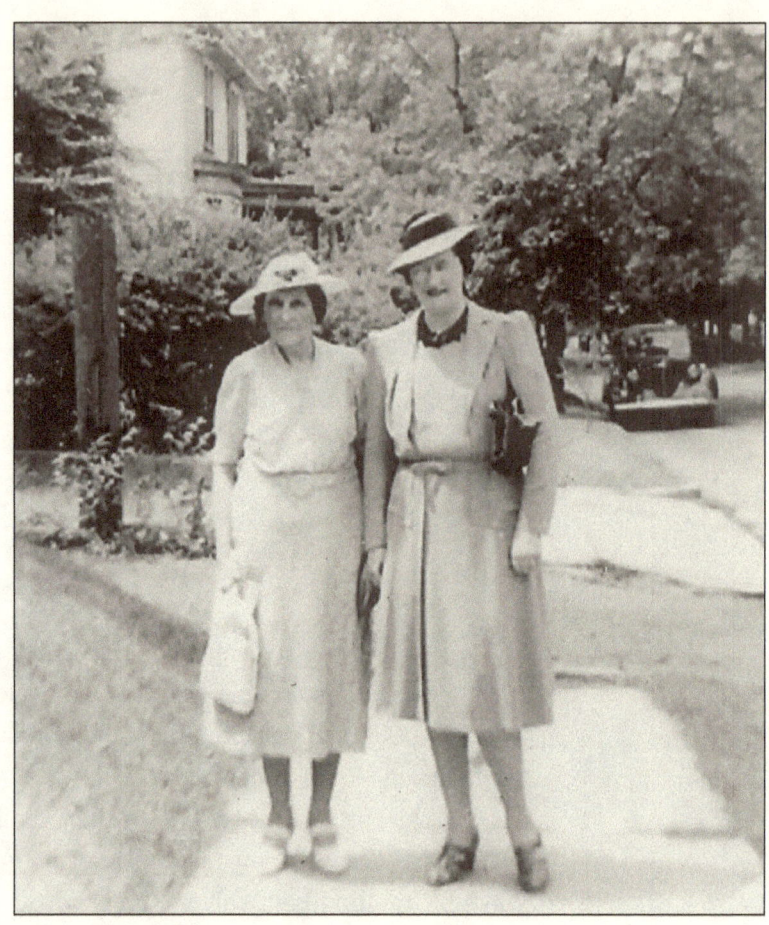

Addie Welker and Margaret Newland, 1946

Bound for Ann Arbor, she anticipated both her education and her job in the university library. "I made a hundred dollars per month with no retirement. We had one fifteen minute break for tea in the afternoon," Marcia said. She was elated by the entire arrangement. The work interested her and the academic environment stimulated her dreams.

The University of Michigan's Library Science program, facilitated by work-study arrangements, created opportunity for a new population to acquire collegiate professional librarianship preparation. The new students included a majority of females, due to wartime reductions of male students. As in many fields, opportunities for women in academic libraries advanced dramatically following those war years and the war's effect on the gender distribution in the student body. Although there were few female professors on campus to be examples, many female students began to think seriously of the possibility of actual careers in the academic environment.

The curriculum plan required year-round part-time course work combined with the library job. Upon completing the Bachelor of Arts degree, the student immediately entered the Master of Arts in Library Science program. The B.A. with her chosen major and minor (English and History) required some specific designated courses. But, beyond those basics, the course catalog offered a bonanza for Marcia. "Since I was working my way through, I took lots of courses in college that had no practical purpose at all. I took Egyptian history, Roman archeology, Greek mythology; many things I really enjoyed. I had a year of Shakespeare which I loved," she said.

"During my time as a student, my days weren't typical student days because I worked in addition to my classes. That work was a part of the program. They were eager to help us get into the university and to succeed. I remember when I was hired, they told me to go and put some belongings in the apartment I was going to share and to apply for a library card so that I could establish residency. The next semester began in November. I arrived promptly and eagerly to begin my formal higher education.

"I was enthralled by the library. I'd never been in one so large. It was eight floors. I was just out of my mind; I loved it. I never saw so many books. I was thrilled to be working in a university. I decided I would stay there until I was seventy.

"Two people I knew who started there at the same time as I did actually did stay until they retired. Michigan had a way of getting into your system. People would retire from there and move into a nearby retirement community so that they never felt they had actually left the university. An older woman there once told me, 'Don't fall into that trap. I did and you shouldn't. It can get so that this is your only life.' It could have been easy to do because the university community had so much to offer—activity, concerts, museums.

"I realized later that it was a very insulated life because all of your friends, your social life, were in the same environment. There might be a few people from town in your church, but otherwise everyone you knew was from the university.

"While I was working, I took six class hours a week. Combining the work with the classes was an excellent way to learn. We were junior librarians and were assigned to a senior librarian. It was possible to apply what we learned immediately."

Insulated though it may have been in some ways, the University of Michigan provided access to experiences that Marcia would have never encountered in Fort Wayne. One recollection illustrates that point. "During World War Two, there was a Japanese Language Institute located there. Part of its purpose was to teach Japanese to military officers. A Japanese librarian was employed to assist with that program. I observed her, but I never knew anything about her as a person. Now I realize that she must have been very lonely. After the war, I recall that the Emperor of Japan came to the Institute and we all lined up for 'inspection' to welcome him. It was all very impressive. Later, Tojo's daughter attended the university. The campus newspaper reminded us that she was not to be blamed for the war and that we should treat her kindly," Marcia said.

In today's terms, that small exposure to the Orient would be characterized as an experience in cultural diversity. For Marcia, it was one piece in a constellation of wonderful things she became a part of in her life in Ann Arbor. "Here I was at a premier university, learning and working and getting the wonderful salary of a hundred dollars a month. I had achieved my life's goal and I was only twenty-three years old! Contrary to what my family had always thought, I was worthy of respect there," she said.

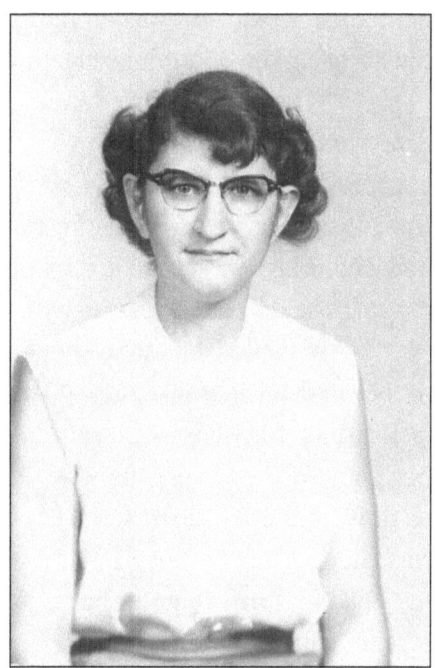

Marcia, 1949

"I became a cataloger and I enjoyed that. In those days it was not done by computer. Humans did it all. I won't say I was an ideal employee. I thought that the rules were too strict. There was only one telephone and we were not permitted to use it for personal calls. But the phone was near the shelf list. I soon found, like everyone else, that you could pretend to be looking something up while making a call. If the supervisor came by, I'd say, 'No, I don't see that listed, but I'll get back to you.' As long as I had a pencil in one hand and some catalog cards in the other, I could go anywhere in the library and look up anything I wanted to read. Imagine!

"If you went through the Depression, you put up with a lot on the job that people today can't imagine. For example, everyone worked in one big room. When a new person began, they were on the side of the room opposite the windows. As you advanced, you got to move to desks nearer the window. It was all rather rigid. But I loved the traditions of the library, even odd things like that.

"When I first started there, a woman who was very elderly and deaf was my supervisor. She called me into her office and asked, 'Do you know Greek and Latin?' I said, 'No, I don't.' She said, 'That's good. I am assigning you Monday to rare books.' She hadn't heard what I had said. Maybe I should just kill myself or leave town, I thought. 'Yes ma'am,' I said. 'Thank you.'

"It turned out that she was a wonderful woman, extremely proper and businesslike. She'd think nothing of assigning you a new task at four fifty-five p.m. From her point of view everyone was on duty until five o'clock. Once I was late to work because I'd hit my head and had to go to have stitches put in. When I arrived, she said, 'Hmmph, I wondered why you were late.' Not a word about my injury—no nonsense. There was nothing warm and fuzzy about her, but she knew her work. She taught me about books. I was so fortunate to be assigned with her for two or three years," Marcia said.

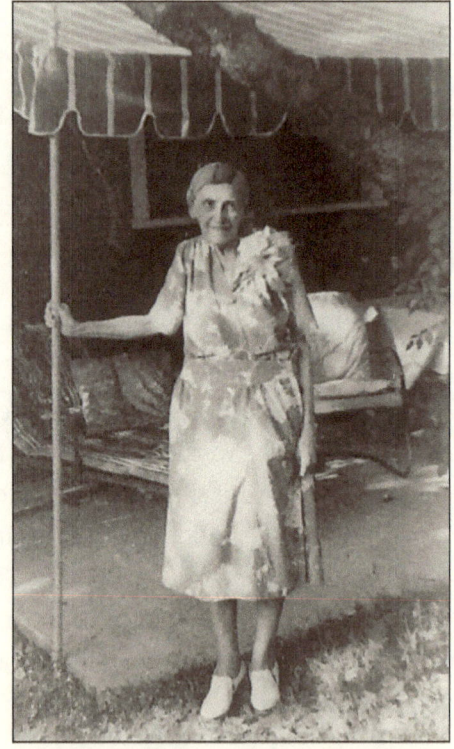

Addie Welker, 1950

Work and classes and exploring the stimulating university environment occupied much of Marcia's time until she completed her B.A. in 1949. She also made time during those years to continue to explore her own creative abilities. She had never stopped writing since childhood. In this encouraging environment, her output increased. She began submitting some of her work for publication. "Before long, as the fifties began, I was publishing poetry regularly in literary magazines and other publications," she said. One poem was published in the magazine *Poet Lore*. That magazine was a respected one that had been published continuously since 1889. Someone told the Head Librarian who was also the Chair of the English Department about her poem's being published. "He sent for me and congratulated me and said I would receive a merit raise of a hundred dollars per year for my literary work. I was thrilled," she said.

Graduate school in Library Science was next on the agenda after Marcia completed her undergraduate degree. She proceeded immediately to enroll and to continue to work in the library as her original commitment to the program prescribed.

Her years on campus had given her the opportunity to find friends who shared her enthusiasm for libraries, literature, and the arts. Her first apartment-mate was a woman she had known from the library in Fort Wayne. Others became close friends, in a few cases partners, for a while. In 1950, she met Allene Schnaitter, who also worked in the general library. Allene was also a graduate student who had enrolled in the Library Science graduate program a year later than Marcia. Their relationship became serious and by 1951 they lived together as partners.

Scene 11

Life and Imagination

> You are in love because of imagination. . . . When we imagine strongly, we begin to fall in love with the images conjured before the heart's eye.
> Hillman, J., *The Soul's Code*, p. 147
>
> The daimon . . . offers comfort and can pull you into its shell but it cannot abide innocence . . . It can make the body ill. It is out of step with time, finding all sorts of faults, gaps, and knots in the flow of life—and it prefers them. Hillman, J., *The Soul's Code*, p. 39

"I just went along because I wasn't as concerned about career as Allene was. She was unhappy because she didn't see any chance for advancement in the general library at University of Michigan where we both worked. Neither one of us was likely to get much increase in pay although we had completed the graduate program in Library Science. The idea was that we should be so happy to be employed there that money would not be all that important. We were supposed to feel the prestige of the institution. From time to time we both would put our names in for consideration for positions elsewhere. Then Allene got one at Antioch University in Yellow Springs, Ohio. So, off we went," Marcia said.

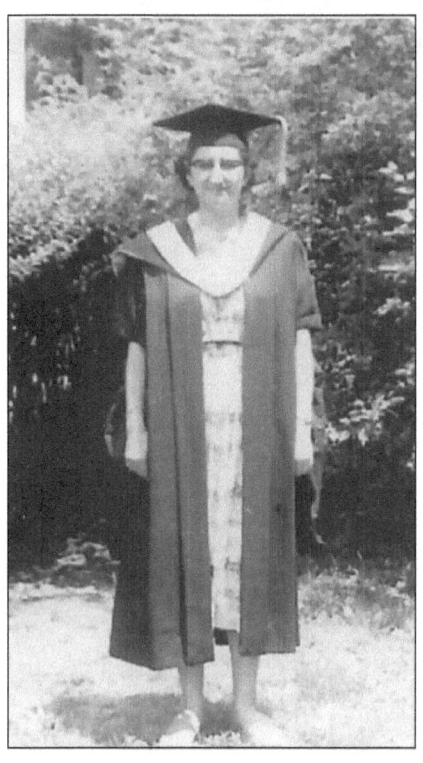

Marcia, receiving Master's Degree at the University of Michigan, 1953

Marcia found a job at the public library in Springfield, Ohio. Before long, Allene was searching again for a university position. Professional advancement was a major concern for her. Marcia's interests in writing made the issue of their location and her position less her major focus. They had been in Ohio less than a year when Allene succeeded in finding a job back in Ann Arbor at the Law Library of the University of Michigan in 1954. They were both happy to return to the community they enjoyed. And, as in the move to Ohio, the couple was following the path of Allene's career aspirations. Marcia had no job waiting when she returned to Michigan.

"I was considered over-qualified for all the library jobs that were available. That kept me out of work for several months. It took me a while, but I got a job as a clerk at the Law Library. I took the clerk position just to get in. I knew that once I was there, I could see what they needed and could show them what I could do. One of the librarians said to me, 'Don't forget, you got in by the back door.' It's true, I did. I've always said that I was 'invited' to come to the Law School. The fact is that I was invited because I continued knocking on the door."

Her eye was on a position that was just being developed, international documents librarian. The fact that the job was new and that the whole area of dealing with international law documents was new for that library was a challenge that intrigued Marcia. She succeeded in being chosen for the new job. "At that time there was no classification system by which to catalog those documents. They weren't included in the Library of Congress system. I invented a system to handle them."

That creative venture earned her a secure niche in the Law Library. Her partner was not effusive in her praise of Marcia's creativity. "Allene's comment was, 'Leave it to you Jews; you come in with a pencil and in a few months you've got an office all your own.'" Marcia said.

"She was anti-Semitic. It did bother me some, but I decided that it was her problem, not mine," Marcia commented. "Her family was very accepting of me. I was always included in family gatherings. Families of the people who I have been partners with were always kind to me."

Some of her own family were less welcoming. "Once when Allene and I went to New York on vacation, we went to visit my father and Olga. At first, he tried to be pleasant. But shortly after, he explained that Olga was uncomfortable with us being there. So we left. I didn't see him for eighteen years after that." The occasional visits from her Aunt Doris and Uncle Lee were not entirely joyous events either. "I always had a nervous stomach that I later figured out coincided with my relatives coming to visit."

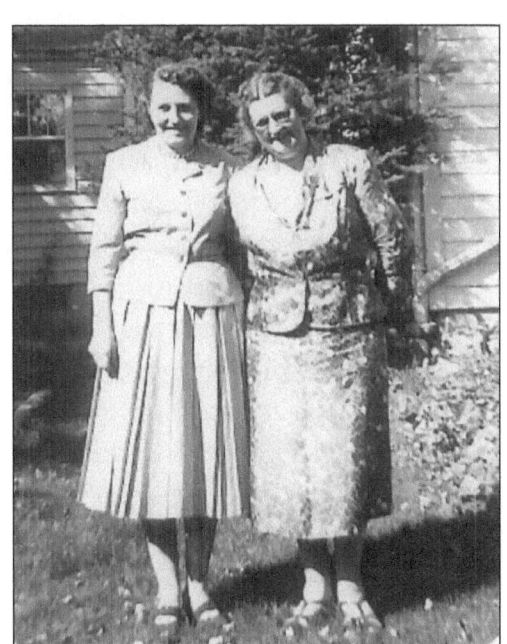

Doris Bernhardt and Margaret
Newland, 1957

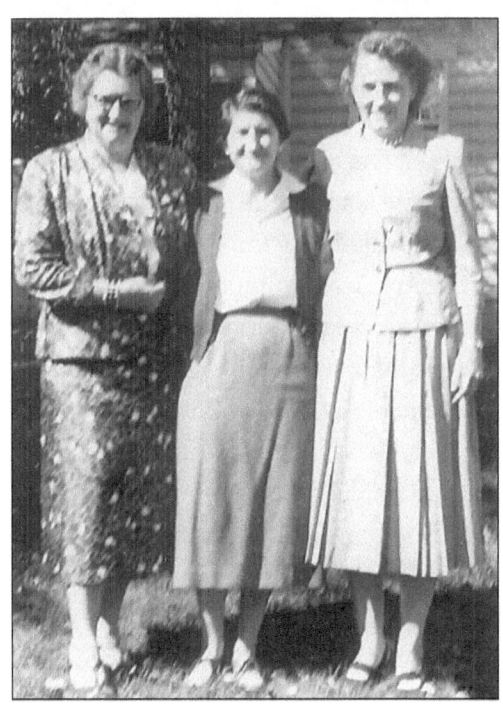

Margaret Newland, Marcia and
Doris Bernhardt, 1957

That stomach complaint resulted in her beginning to explore a new type of creative expression in addition to her writing. "I went to the doctor about my stomach. He told me I needed a hobby. He suggested making models—miniature cars or planes. I'm no good at making tiny things, so it came to me—I don't know if I read about serigraphs or saw an exhibit—I decided I would make silk screen prints.

"I bought a kit and learned how to make abstract prints. Then I joined an art club that a neighbor belonged to. We met once a week and had a professor from the college come in to critique our work. It was very helpful to be in that group.

"As a chance meeting when I was out walking one day, I ran into a woman who was the sister of a person I had known in school. We talked and I learned that her husband was a maker of artificial limbs. We became friendly because they lived down the street. Later I told him that I wanted to be able to make larger prints than I could make with the frames from the kit I had bought. He told me that he could make me some. And he did—several different-sized silk screen boxes. I set up all my equipment in a studio that I made in a space in the basement of the house we lived in.

"The art group had an exhibit and some of my prints sold. I had also made some cards of the prints and people bought those also. I can't say that Allene encouraged me, but it kept me busy. I joined the Ann Arbor Art Association. The members were mostly professional artists and some creative amateurs like me. We were encouraged to enter a contest held in conjunction with the Fiftieth Anniversary of the Detroit Museum of Art. One of my prints was chosen for the show. We received two tickets for the dinner at the museum and my name was listed in the little catalog of the exhibit. That gave me more standing in the art group in Ann Arbor. That was a big thrill. I felt encouraged, but I didn't think of myself as an artist. I thought a person couldn't be a real artist if she hadn't gone to art school and if she couldn't draw."

As the 1960s began, Allene had again decided that a job change was important for her. "From the beginning, our relationship was built on the premise that she was smarter, better-educated and had the better job. Until we both had jobs at the law school, usually that was the case. But that changed because she was an assistant and there was no likelihood she was going to move up," Marcia said. "I was very happy in my job. Allene was not happy because she was being passed over for promotions. I probably could have stayed there all my life. For technical reasons, I probably should have because I'd already gotten my certification as a law librarian."

Satisfying Allene's desire for a different situation, they found positions at the University of Missouri in Columbia, Missouri, beginning in 1961. Marcia was in the Law Library. "I liked Missouri also. I had this ideal view of what a wonderful life would be. It would be to work and live in a small college in a small college town. I'd stay on there and live there even after I retired. I love small towns and the Midwest. Columbia seemed like it would fit that ideal. Unfortunately, I later realized that the climate there was bad for my health and would have killed me to stay there," Marcia said.

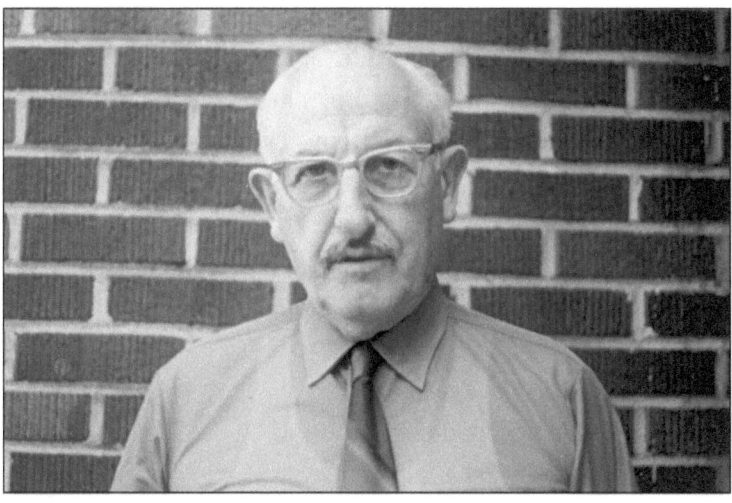

Frank Miller, 1965

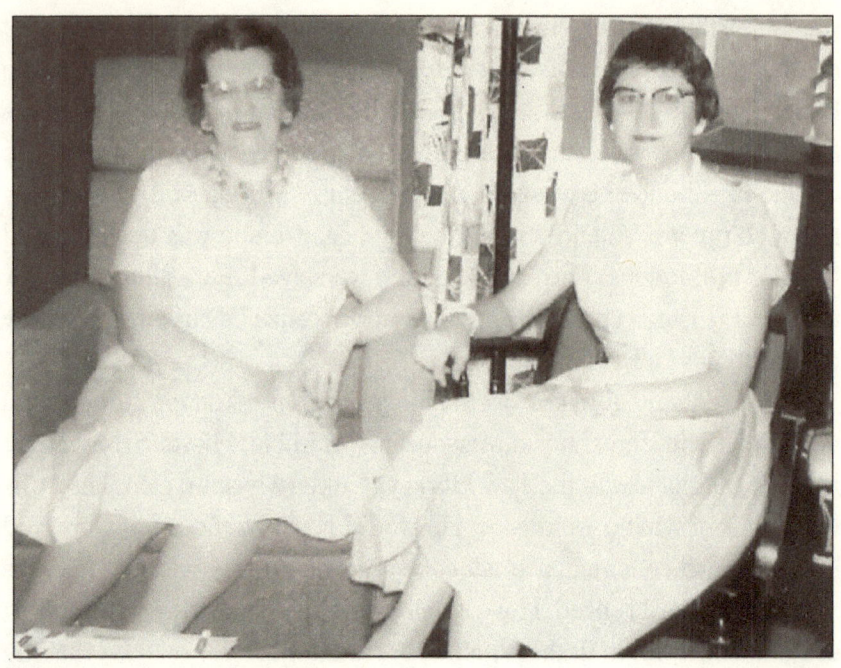

Marcia with Mother, 1964

She continued making prints, again in a basement studio that she set up in their Missouri house. But, she began to feel torn between the art work and her writing. The physical work involved in making the prints also began to cause problems with her hands. Bit by bit, she reduced her print work and increased her writing. Her poems continued being published frequently in well-known publications. "To Accept the Laurel" was in a 1966 edition of *Arizona Quarterly*.

> To accept the laurel
> is to accept defeat
> Of self-cast anonymity;
> To step aside, even once
> Is to lose nonentity of face

Breeding hatred in the faceless.
The rite of crowning proclaims
The right of destruction;
Hidden in the green leaves,
The gold filigree, the worm
That turns and eats to the quick.

Good poetry transcends, offering meaning beyond that which originally prompted its creation by the poet. Since no annotation accompanies that poem, the experience that evoked it isn't clear. But, Marcia's life was changing at that time. Allene again aimed for professional advancement. She planned to return to graduate school for a Ph.D. "By that time, there wasn't much glamour left in our relationship. She was interested in going to school and moving up in her career while I was happy with my job and my writing and print-making. We had reached the point that for over a year we had been just friends. That part was because she also was interested in a more adventurous life. I was pretty dull," Marcia said.

Marcia in Her Study, Columbia, Missouri, 1966

Trying Santa Fe

> The acorn acts less as a personal guide with a sure
> long-term direction than a moving style, an inner
> dynamic that gives the feeling of purpose to occasion
> . . . Let's say the acorn is more concerned with the
> soul aspect of events, more alive to what's good for it
> than to what you believe is good for you.
> Hillman, J., *The Soul's Code*, p. 203

The co-owner of the Villagra Bookstore near Santa Fe, New Mexico's plaza noticed the new customer, a short woman with dark hair. Noticing her as she browsed, Roslyn Eisenberg thought that she was probably from out of town; maybe a librarian. "Her appearance now is much more relaxed," Roslyn said of the woman who has now been her friend for nearly forty years. "She was dressed in a skirt, blouse and jacket and I recall that she seemed a bit shy but perhaps interested in finding friends." Their mutual love of books created a bond that expanded. "We're like family now. We live near one another and visit at least weekly. I often watch Marcia paint while we visit."

One of Marcia's paintings, *Villagra Bookstore*, is based on the store where she found her new friend. Although she first visited Eisenberg's store in the 1960s, she created a 1930s version of that establishment for the painting. Applying her memory painting style and imagination to the store resulted in a view of a cheerful place full of customers dressed in typical clothes of that time. Eleven adults and six children shop among titles from the 1930s. *Brave New World, The Great Gatsby,* and Willa Cather titles are shelved among works on the history and culture of the Southwest. Children consider *Mother Goose* and *Treasure Island.* Multicolored hollyhocks blooming outside the windows flanking the sales counter say it is summer here. Pottery pieces in the various styles of several New Mexico pueblos rest atop the bookshelves and a kiva-style fireplace awaits the chill of fall. "It makes me smile," Eisenberg said of the painting which is a part of her personal collection.

⊨ ⊨ ⊨

Newton's First Law of Motion, the so-called Law of Inertia, states that every object in a state of uniform motion tends to remain in that state of motion unless an external force is applied to it. Simply stated, a thing tends to keep doing what it is doing until something intervenes—rolling along or standing still—it just keeps on. People are more complex than inanimate objects, but the same principle seems to apply. In Marcia Muth's case, she rolled along or perhaps seemed to stand still, in Columbia, Missouri for nearly six years. And then in 1966, something overcame inertia, changed her direction and state of motion. Actually, several things seemed to converge. Repeated pulmonary illnesses—bronchitis and pneumonia—prompted her physician to urge her to move to a less humid climate. But her companion, Allene, began making changes in her own life, planning to return to graduate school for her Ph.D. "She wanted more adventure. I wasn't interested in going to bars or the things she became interested in doing. I suppose I've always been a bit of a prude. I don't drink hard liquor or serve it to guests. So, a lot of our interests were no longer the same. And we had just been good friends, as I've said, nothing more, for a long time." Marcia's work at the University of Missouri Law Library had begun to become too familiar. And then there's the acorn that may have begun urging something that would be good for IT.

Whatever the forces at work, Marcia was impelled. Explaining her choice of Santa Fe, she said, "I knew this area a bit from having been a visitor and I knew some people here. I wrote that I was thinking of making a change." Dr. Jean Rosenbaum and his wife Veryl were her acquaintances because he had included some of her poetry in a collection he had published. Rosenbaum, a psychiatrist and psychoanalyst, had several writer friends in the area to whom he and his wife introduced Marcia.

Her primary literary efforts had been focused on poetry since she had concluded some years before that she wasn't ever going to be a very good novelist. The prospect of associating with a group with similar interests in the arts, including several poets, appealed to Marcia. "They wrote and said that there was a new state library building going up. I came out and applied for a job and was accepted. Allene drove me out here. I was never a great driver and wouldn't have driven all the way alone. So, she drove me out here and flew back. She went off to get her Ph.D. at the University of Indiana and after that had some adventurous years in Chicago. She sold the house we had owned in Columbia and I took my part to eventually buy a house here."

During the years in Columbia, Marcia had refined her abilities as a poet. She was frequently published in popular venues such as *The Christian Science Monitor* as well as in the poetry series of some academic presses. The *Arizona Quarterly* carried several, including notes about the author. The descriptions track her movement. In 1966, the captions described her as Assistant Law Librarian at the University of Missouri. A 1967 note said she had been published widely in a variety of periodicals. Santa Fe appeared as her new location in a 1968 issue. Her poems are free verse—unrhymed, adhering to no specific line length—a favorite scheme of Walt Whitman and Robert Frost. A poet who is less interested in experiments with form than with meaning, she wrote pieces full of clear images and crisp language. "My poetry, there may be hidden meanings there if you look for them but basically, anybody could get something out of it," she said. No single subject predominated in those verses. Together they tend to suggest that the poet is an observer, an absorber and translator of experiences that are common to many. And she was known at the time by her full name, Marcia Muth Miller. "Lazarus Revisited," published in the *Arizona Quarterly* in 1966, exemplifies her tone and style.

> To come from the dead is hard
> To live again is harder still
> All sores healed, all sorrows gone;
> Having slept that sleep of content
> No dark or light to hurt the eye.
> Now thrust again into this world
> A sudden return, a second birth;
> The pain of life comes back
> As hunger, thirst, desire take hold.

Continuing success as a poet, new friends in Santa Fe, and the community of writers with whom she associated pleased her. But she missed the academic environment. Looking back from Santa Fe, she recalled a vitality in Columbia that she hadn't yet found in her life in the new environment. Her day job's activities just didn't match the constant stream of students and professors in search of arcane legal precedents back at the University Law Library. She decided to leave Santa Fe and return to Missouri. She began to collect her belongings to pack.

Friends invited her to dinner, mentioning they wanted her to meet a mutual friend. Maybe she thought, "Well, I do have to eat." She accepted the invitation and held off on the packing.

She's Wonderful! She's A Poet

What heartsease and bliss in finding a corresponding soul who singles us out! How long we move about, desperate to discover someone who can really see us, tell us who we are. Hillman, J., *The Soul's Code*, p. 163

She's almost constantly moving; her fluid grace and erect bearing belie her eighty-two years. Sitting still is not a natural state for this small woman. But, she settled after being convinced that to know something of her is to know more of Marcia. Jody Ellis, Marcia Muth's partner of forty years, began to tell of their first meeting, then interrupted herself to ask, "Would you like some coffee?" Assured that no one needed tending to, she began again. "Some friends said, 'Let's have dinner. We know someone you might like to meet.' I said, 'That's good for me.' We had dinner and I just knew right away. I thought she was wonderful. She was a poet and a totally all-round wonderful person. So I told her how I felt.

And I said, 'I'm not here and there. If you really like me and would like to be partners, it would be forever.' She said, 'Let me think about it.' I said, 'You love Missouri and have a lot of years there. But I have to be here in Santa Fe. It's the place for me. So you also think about whether you want to go back to Missouri.'

"At the time I worked at the Game and Fish Department for the State of New Mexico. Marcia worked right across the street, but we had never met. The next day I called her. She said that she thought this would be a very nice relationship, so 'yes.'"

Jody paused a second and smiled at the memory from 1967, the year that she was 42 and Marcia was 48. "I had lived a lot of my childhood with my grandparents. That's one thing that we had in common. I think it resulted in both of us being, in our own ways, very disciplined. I was with them because my parents had divorced and all that.

"My mother was a legal stenographer and my stepfather was a structural engineer. They had worked, traveling around, for companies that built military bases during the war years. They had worked at Los Alamos. Afterward, in the late nineteen forties, they settled in Santa Fe. People who have lived in Los Alamos call that 'coming back downhill.' About that time I was talking with my mother who asked if I'd thought of living in Santa Fe. So, I came to visit. They lived on East Garcia. It was all different then. Santa Fe was a village. It had something wonderful. The minute I walked down the street and smelled the air and saw the sky and the blue, I thought, 'I must have come up from the ground here because I just adore it.' No matter how it changes, it doesn't change me."

Knowing she would return to Santa Fe because she felt so completely attached to it, she decided to go away to college. "I planned to be in the theater. So I began studying speech and drama. But it didn't work out. I got sick with rheumatic fever and had to be in the hospital.

"After being in the hospital, I liked it so well I decided to go to nursing school. When I finished, I was back here in Santa Fe for a while and did some private duty, mostly geriatrics. Then I went into the Air Force for three years, during Korea."

A photo of Nurse Lieutenant Jody in uniform hangs on a wall in their home office. In it she seemed even tinier than her current "barely five feet." Explaining why she left nursing after her tour in the Air Force, she said, "I'd had enough. I'm not very big or physically strong, even though I am wiry. Nursing was hard physical work."

Instead, she became a Santa Fe confectioner on Palace Avenue, across from St. Francis Cathedral. "I had mustering out pay of about two hundred fifty dollars, which was a lot back then. The people who owned the shop had priced it around ten thousand dollars, I think. But, they took what I had and said, 'Just pay a little at a time, as you can.' People weren't as greedy back then. All the candy was made right there. I enjoyed that, but after about three years, I became very sick and had to have a thyroidectomy. So, I had to give it up. After that, I did a lot of different things. I've always been able to make a living because I work hard and am able to do a lot of things."

She sped through the account of her own history, almost dismissing it as entirely unimportant. "This is about Marcia, not me. All of this is old stuff," she said, laughing. She preferred to focus on the present and preferably not on herself, even though her accomplishments are extensive and she is a very respected member of the Santa Fe community.

After a pause during which she answered a telephone call from one of her cello students and checked to see if Marcia needed anything while she painted, she returned. Asked to describe how she and Marcia affect one another, she said, "Marcia is a very strong individual. She's almost hard on herself because she's strict with herself. I'm very outgoing, sort of 'gooey,' *espressivo* as we say in music. Marcia's much more within herself, introspective."

Exploring the idea of those differences, Jody agreed that those are very different temperaments that could easily be oppositional. "But, we have similar opinions, think alike on most subjects. We support one another. It was just meant to be, maybe chemistry, I don't know. Something clicked all those years ago and never came unglued.

"I like to take care of her and as long as we live, I will. It's kind of like adhesive tape," she said. "Even though I say that I take care of her, I think our relationship is pretty much fifty-fifty. I depend a lot on her too. She has the more logical mind.

"Another thing that we agree on and live by is that a person should never lose a childlike quality, should play every day. And we do."

Asked her assessment of Jody, Marcia's response—obviously a line she's used before, delivered deadpan—was, "She's my greatest fan. We both worship the ground I walk on." She rolled her eyes and laughed. The interviewer had been made a part of a game.

up To and Able—Inventing Sunstone

> Goals too clearly defined can become blinkers.
> Bateson, M., *Composing a Life*, p. 6-7

"Marcia was working at the State Library and I was working at Game and Fish. We had state jobs and they weren't high paying, so money for us was a little tight. Sometimes it was tough," Jody said. "One day she called during work and said, 'How would you like to go into business?'

"I said, 'Why not?' I was kind of kidding, but then I realized she wasn't. Well, I was up for anything because she has such a wonderful head on her shoulders and had such a strong logical mind—looking ahead.

"She said, 'Okay, we're going into the research and ghost writing business.' So we did. We called it Ellis Research Associates. That's how all of that got started."

Marcia recalled that they started the business with capitalization of forty-five dollars—all they had to spare. "We bought stationery and had business cards printed. Back then there were no computers, so all we wrote, we typed manually and all the research was done first-hand.

"It began simply enough. A local politician was going to speak to the League of Women Voters. His people brought him over so I could listen to him and then I wrote him a speech. Someone else was speaking to a Bible class. We were very ecumenical. And we could see the possibilities. These people were lazy! We named the business Ellis Research Associates because at first I was still working at the State Library and we thought that might not be looked on too well.

"Pretty soon we got enough work that I quit my job and next Jody quit hers. I did the writing and she did the typing and helped with the research. Later we hired other typists, too. We even had an ad in *Atlantic Monthly*. I can't tell you how many theses we finished for people. We had this lady once who was an historian. She had written a book—well, she had all the notes—and then she got sick. She found out about us and made an appointment to meet us. She told us to meet her at a particular gas station. She arrived with a suitcase full of material, none of it organized. She had us correspond with her in a plain envelope without our business name so that no one would know.

"I ghost wrote for our friend, Dr. Rosenbaum, too. He said to me, 'I always wanted to write something about psychology for the public, but I just can't seem to get it out. Why don't we work on something together under my name? You'll get fifty percent of anything we make.' For a few months, I had to work closely with him to learn his style. He was a Freudian. One day he noticed a book about Jung on my bookshelf. He was concerned I might get contaminated by the ideas in it. I'd never even read it.

"We got a contract with a publisher for the first book. It was called *Practical Psychiatry*. The next one was *Your Volkswagen, the Sex Symbol*. He became very popular because of those—was on television on the Today Show. After a while, he told me, 'You're a wonderful writing machine.' We did another book that I wrote entirely. It was about psychosomatic medicine, something that has always interested me. The title was *The Mind Factor*. He promised me I could be listed as co-author. But even though the publishing company knew I was the ghost writer, they said no. They had their eye on the pocketbook. They were concerned that the public wouldn't buy the book because my name was unknown in the field and I wasn't a doctor. The only thing that Dr. Rosenbaum actually contributed to that book was his name. By that time I knew how to write all that mush, including all the case histories. They were people I knew or had made up. It was all logic and common sense.

"With the popularity of those books and the related publicity, we then did a lot of articles for the *National Enquirer*." She laughed as she recalled the method for developing subjects for those articles. "We had all our friends come up with ideas for subjects or questions the articles would answer. If the idea was used by the *Enquirer*, then we paid them ten dollars for the idea. We had to present ten ideas for possible topics each week. I was fortunate because this was all common sense to me. If I needed to do any research, I'd go to the library. If not, I'd just write it."

Those were the days when the *Enquirer* was the tabloid competition for the popular movie magazines. It carried many articles on celebrities' lives and entertained the readers with pop psychology furnished by the ghosts in Santa Fe. Fortunately, UFOs and extraterrestrial visitations were not yet a staple of its pages. Otherwise, Ellis Research Associates might have needed to spend time studying the mysterious events near Roswell.

"All this time, Marcia was writing poetry. It was the most beautiful stuff. I'd never read much poetry in my life, except in school. But hers, I could really understand. I admired that she could just sit down in the middle of the night and write something. And for me, it was so fascinating to be a part of all of that," Jody said.

Poems from 1969 and 1970 published in the *Arizona Quarterly* offer a view of the range of subjects addressed by Marcia Muth Miller in those days. The first, "After the Dreams," speaks to a topic of continuing interest to Marcia, dreams.

> These are things of the subconscious
> dragged back into reality
> for our reluctant examination;
> we turn the limp forms over
> with trembling hands. Curious.
> They lie dying in the coolness
> of the ordinary morning.

"I wrote something once about the people whom I'd never met who were in my dreams. I wondered if these people were in my dreams, was I in some one else's dreams too," she said.

Observation of nature, as in "Summer," is also a recurring theme in her poetry.

> We are caught here
> in summer's thrall
> caught,
> caught by bird song
> by grass-smell air
> and insect sound;
> by time
> time slowed to match a sun
> whose long drive
> stretches
> early morning to later night.

Humans' affecting natural beauty and the resulting loss of wonder and grandeur were poignantly caught in "Postcard Views and Other Souvenirs."

> The night-formed crescent of moon
> Swims like an odd fish in our starred sky,
> This borrowed light that swells and fades
> To mark our calendar of time
> Is now within our mortal reach;
> I sorrow for beauty being made familiar,
> Another cathedral for visiting, littering, and defacing.

⚡ ⚡ ⚡

"I thought somebody besides me should get to appreciate her poetry. I said, 'Why don't we make a little booklet that can contain your poetry?' We talked about it and about how there were so many wonderful poets, photographers, writers, and essayists in Santa Fe. They were what we called 'Santa Fe Characters.' I thought someone ought to notice them. So we put out the word that we were planning to do something like that. Pretty soon we had a plan and we had started the *Sunstone Review*," Jody said.

The *Sunstone Review* became the first literary magazine of Santa Fe, joining only a few "little magazines" of its sort published outside academic settings in the United States at that time. The plan was to showcase the work of poets and other literary artists who were from Santa Fe and the Southwest or whose work reflected themes relevant to the region. Publication began with the first issue in 1971. The price was $1.50 per issue or $5.00 for an annual subscription of four issues. A new adventure had begun.

Change and Excitement

All too often men and women are like battered wives or abused children. We hold on to the continuity we have, however profoundly it is flawed. If change were less frightening, if the risk did not seem so great, far more could be lived. Bateson, M., *Composing a Life*, p. 78

Neither Marcia nor Jody was bound by a strong concern for maintaining the continuity that their "day jobs" had offered. The success of their ghost writing business made letting go and moving on to other ventures seem the only logical choice.

Branching out to begin *Sunstone Review* combined all the ingredients for an exciting next phase. Interacting with writers and artists, assembling an editorial board, and encouraging their own creative work and that of others demanded their full-time commitment. Gaining financial support for the enterprise demanded their attention too. Some friends and acquaintances assisted by becoming patrons of the *Sunstone Review*.

One provided a subscription to the *Review* for the libraries at all the state universities in the United States. That quickly broadened the audience, assuring readership outside the usual "Santa Fe Characters." Before long, poetry and other work were arriving over the transom from authors across the nation seeking publication in the new literary magazine.

Among the other early patrons were two people who became friends and eventually business associates. "We lived on the East Side and the house next door was rented for the summer to a singer with the Santa Fe Opera. I went to a conference somewhere, Philadelphia, I think. Before I left, I said to Jody, 'Don't bother that opera guy that moved in there.' While I was at the conference Jody and I talked by phone and she said she'd met him and he came over and had breakfast." So much for not bothering the neighbor.

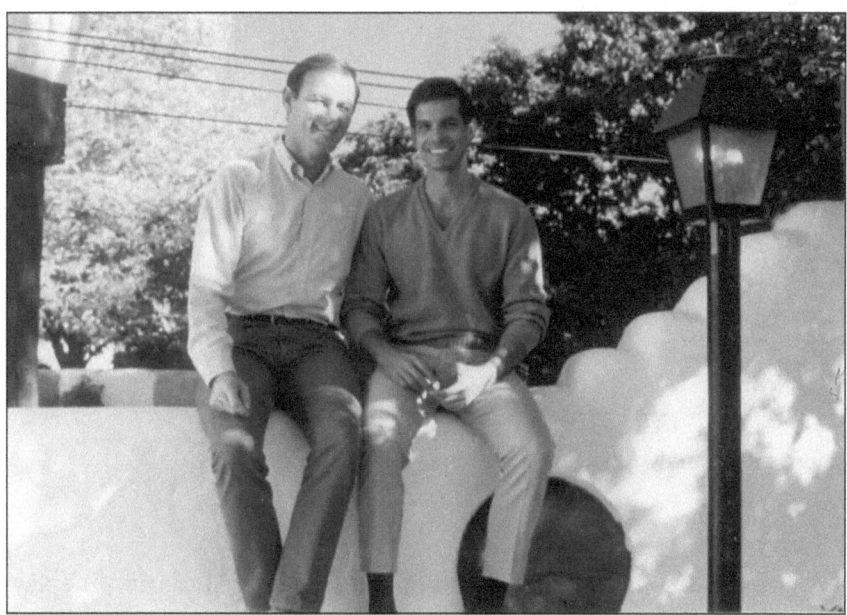

John Reardon, James Smith, 1968

The "opera guy" was John Reardon, a well-known operatic baritone from New York City's Metropolitan Opera. He was in Santa Fe to perform at the Santa Fe Opera during its summer season under the stars. Reardon's publicist, James Clois Smith, Jr., was the next new neighbor that the women from Sunstone met and befriended. "I remember this little woman looking over the fence at me in the backyard one day. She beckoned me over and invited me to come and have coffee," Jim Smith said. Marcia recalled Smith wearing white shoes and a light colored suit and being "very good looking."

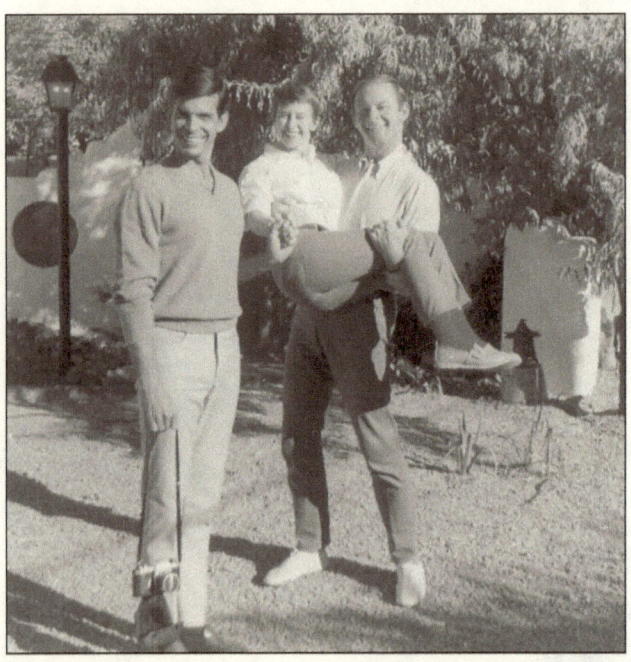

James Smith, Jody Ellis, John Reardon, 1968

"That summer John would go out to the opera during the day, rehearsing, and we four would socialize some in the evenings. John was very devoted to his mother. She came out for a while and Jody's stepfather had moved here. They were both Christian Scientists, so we got them together a few times. We all became friends," Marcia said. Jim was listed, along with Dr. Rosenbaum, of popular psychology fame, as one of the *Review's* patrons in its first issue. When Reardon and Smith returned to New York after Santa Fe's opera season, they kept in contact.

As the *Review* became a reality, its pages included poems by several poets whose works were found in other publications in subsequent years. May Sarton was one of the more widely known whose work joined that of Adelaide Bloomfield, Jean Burroughs, Peggy Church, Peter Dechert, and Joanna Carlson, among many others. And poems by Marcia Muth Miller were included in the new showcase for her work that Jody had hoped for.

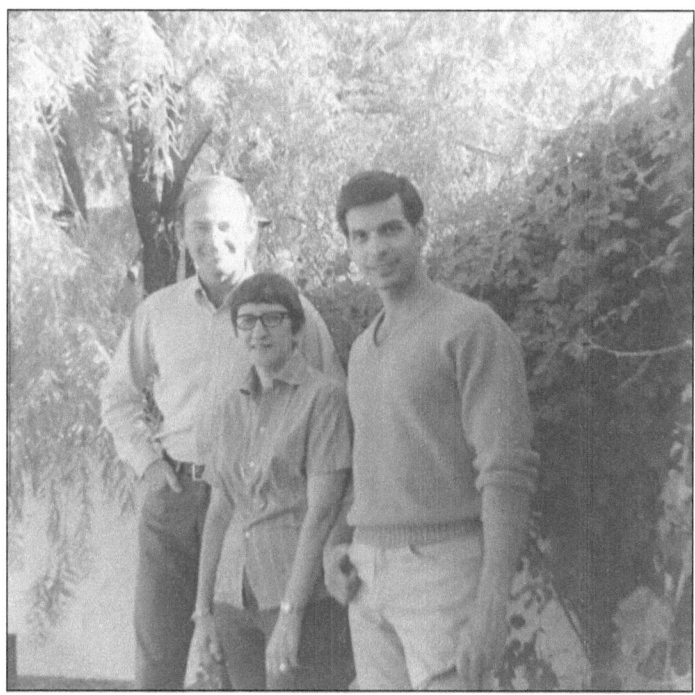

John Reardon, Marcia, James Smith, 1968

An issue of the *Review* from 1972 gives a clue to the fact that the early 1970s were a period of intense activity for Marcia and Jody. Sunstone Press is listed as the publisher of a book of poetry mentioned in that issue. Sunstone Press was created as a natural adjunct to the *Review*. In addition to publishing poetry, the company's mission was to spotlight work about the Southwest Region. Just as with their other business development, the Press was begun on little more than a shoestring. Aside from the relatively small amount of money Marcia and Jody had available to invest and the large investment of creative and business talent they provided, there was relatively little available to capitalize the new business entity. In order to create a firmer base for operations, Sunstone Press was incorporated and some stock was sold.

Among the stockholders, in addition to founders Marcia and Jody, were John Reardon and Jim Smith. Another investor was Fred Rogers, who had been a college classmate of John Reardon's at Rollins College in Florida. Rogers became a well known figure in Public Television with his long-running children's program, Mister Rogers' Neighborhood.

Only those who have developed a business from idea through to operation can imagine the excitement and hard work that those years held. At the ages of 52 and 46, Marcia and Jody accomplished workloads usually expected of much younger entrepreneurs. Success seemed to generate energy. Jody recalled something of the intense activity during those years. "We did everything. Besides the editorial and related work, we sold our books and we traveled around Northern New Mexico and parts of Colorado selling our wares."

Ma Frump made her debut in 1972, with Sunstone's publication of a small book entitled *Ma Frump's Cultural Guide to Plastic Gardening*. Author Frump was none other than Marcia Muth Miller. Known among her friends for her tireless cultivation of plastic plants, the master plastic gardener shared her knowledge in the book, which enjoyed an audience large enough to require a second edition the following year. For $2.00, the reader could receive such guidance as, "Garden loveliness is the term I use to describe the garden which has more than plastic flowers in it. I am talking now about those lovely gardens which are filled with plastic statuary, fences and other accessories . . . I remember one beautiful garden I visited which had a life-sized reproduction of the famed Winged Victory, done in gold plastic and standing in a bed of plastic daisies. The effect was quite overwhelming." Advice abounds, clearly drawn from real life because the yard of her home today continues to feature plastic plants along with numerous pink plastic flamingos and a miniature G.I. Joe scaling a small boulder. An addition that attests to her ability to change with the times is the use of rainbow-hued computer disks blossoming in the winter-bare trees.

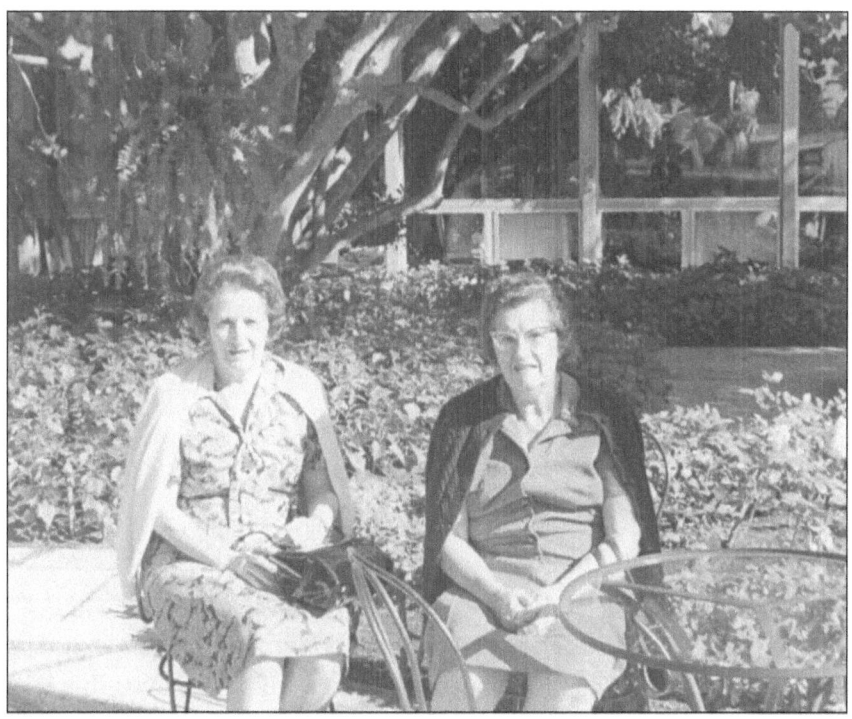

Doris Bernhardt and Margaret Newland, 1969

Ma Frump followed the success of that book with *Ma Frump's Cultural Guide to Instant Intellectualism.* The same satirical tone as in the prior book offered a send-up of those whose hallmark is the superficiality of their intellectual grasp. A survey of methods (phrases to use, home décor to suggest ones intellectual interests) and applications (everyday uses of Zen and astrology) explore the subject, superficially. Perhaps she capitalized on a trend she had detected. And perhaps she, too, had now qualified as a genuine Santa Fe Character.

⊱ ⊱ ⊱

The work necessary to produce the *Review* and the books from Sunstone Press soon required a larger work force. Marcia planned a way to accomplish all that work and to do it from their home. "We built a house. We started to build a small house, but enlarged it to about thirty-two hundred square feet. It had a garage that we rented to the company. That was Sunstone's warehouse. In those days, you had to have a typesetter, a darkroom and someone to do the bills. We had someone to wrap packages because we had a steady mail-order business. The actual printing was done in Albuquerque, but everything up to that was done right there in our home. Eventually we had ten employees. We paid them all. We didn't pay much, but we made enough to meet our payroll.

"Pretty soon that got to be a pain. They'd go into the house and help themselves. It just got to be too much. And I said, 'It's time they move out.' I looked in the paper and found a place that was for rent. I think it was three hundred fifty dollars per month. It had been Ruby's Nursing Home at one time. That was before any of the newer hotels were downtown. It was mostly just pensioners who lived down there."

That location at 239 Johnson Street is the one still occupied by Sunstone Press in 2007. The building, now owned by Jim Smith, is just a few doors west of the Georgia O'Keeffe Museum and across the street from the Eldorado Hotel. Downtown Santa Fe has changed as Sunstone Press continues.

In its third year, the *Sunstone Review* included a slight change of focus, moving from primarily poetry to "dedicated to the arts," a broader perspective that brought more photographs and critical reviews to its pages. In 1973, an issue's back page carried some paid advertising and a listing of the Sunstone Press catalog of books—eighteen titles. Subsequent change was marked by a new design and layout that was first used in 1974. In that same year, poetry in the *Review* by Marcia Muth Miller carried a byline stating that her work had appeared in the *Arizona Quarterly*, *Colorado State Review*, *Poetry Bag*, and the *Christian Science Monitor*. "I liked having pieces in the *Christian Science Monitor* because they paid for them," she said.

Despite all the work of operating a developing business, Marcia's output of poetry continued. And that poetry was well received, admired by many. The volume entitled *Post Card Views and Other Souvenirs*, published in 1973, contains a foreword by Prewitt Edelman which describes the appeal of her poetry. "In a time when much poetry has either gone underground, confusing craft with inarticulation, or has irrevocably locked itself into the airtight rooms of Academe, there are a few men and women—a very few—whose writing sustain the old, time-honored concept of poetry as the making of a verbal object. One of those few is Marcia Muth Miller, whose poetry comes as close as any I know to the Frost tradition." An example of her poetry from that period, in that volume, is "Hall of the American Indian—Third Floor, North Wing."

> In the museum, I walked through the Hall
> Of Indian baskets, weapons, color lithographs
> Of the old chiefs, warriors and their horses;
> I looked at their proud eyes that trusted

The itinerant artists to record the truth,
Yet the truth betrayed is what covers the face
Of chief and time alike. These are remnants,
Clever symbols locked in and under glass,
"Do not touch" reads the crooked printed sign
But it is now three hundred years too late

⊨ ⊨ ⊨

Frank Miller and Marcia had not seen one another in the years between 1953 and 1971. One of their last contacts had been during a vacation she and Allene had taken during which they had visited him and his wife Olga. Olga's reception made clear her disapproval of Marcia's style of life. Frank had not intervened. Following that, for eighteen years neither father nor daughter contacted the other.

There are no author's notes to suggest a connection between that period and her poem "At The Rummage Sale." A reader knowing of the rift between the two might wonder.

Someone's ancestor he must have been, I suppose
Now fourth or fifth-handed cast upon the rummage drift
Of old clothes, books, pictures, assorted dishes
Odd-lotted from the cupboards of dying households;
I buy him for myself with an air of thievery
If my own I do not know, I shall make
My past, like God, in my own likeness as I wish it.

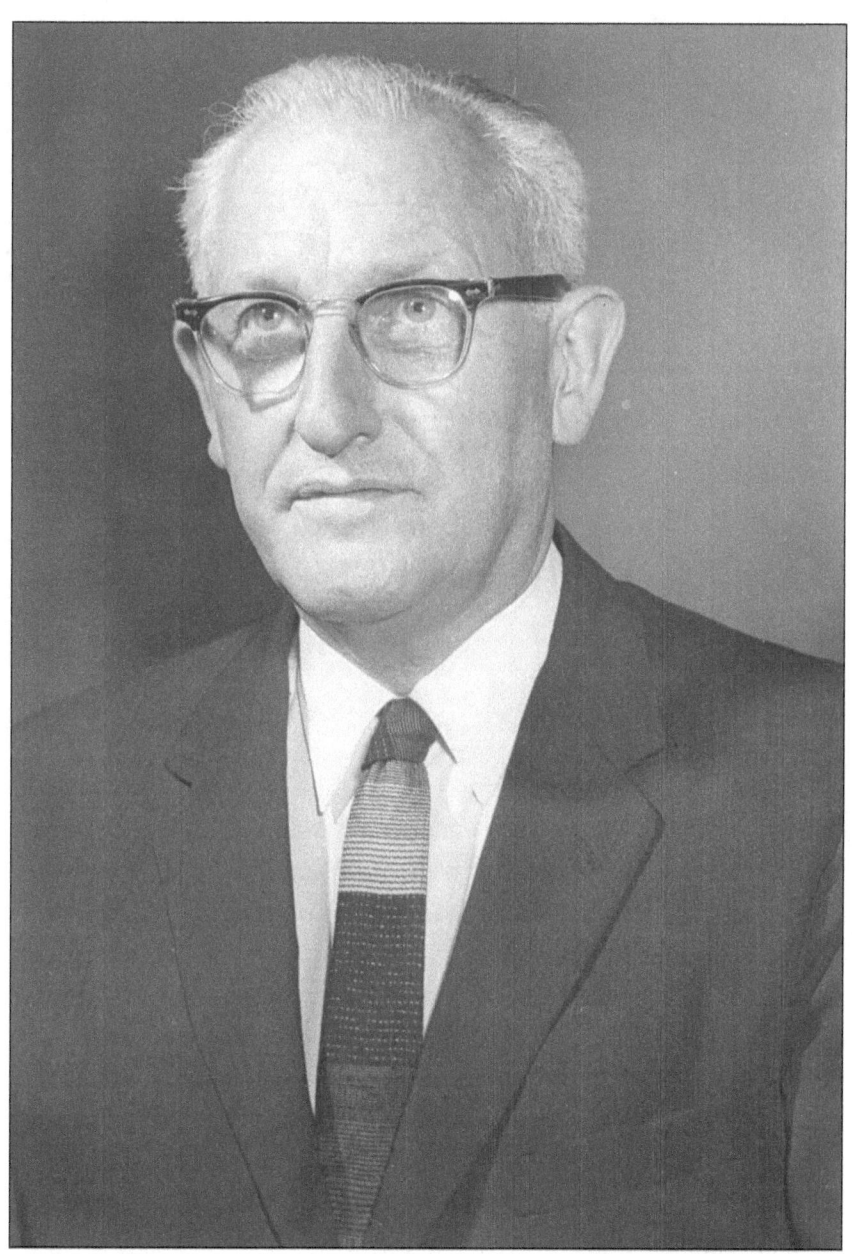

Frank Miller, 1969

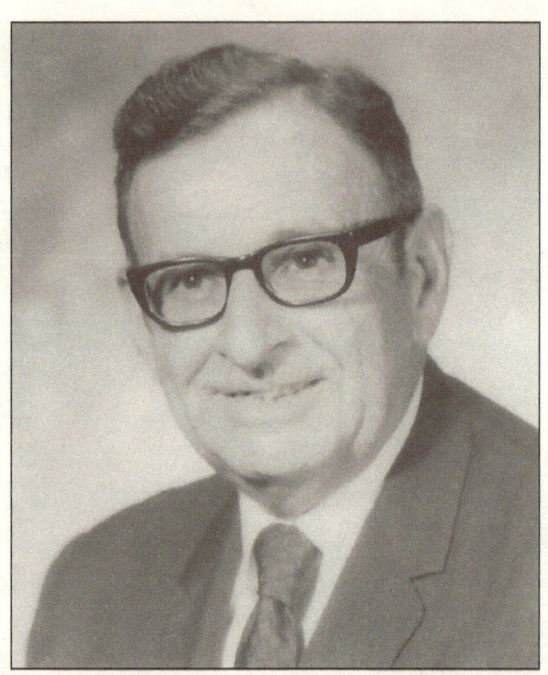

Lee Bernhardt, 1970

In 1971, on her father's birthday, Marcia commented to Jody, "He will be seventy now." Jody encouraged Marcia to get in touch with him. She did and he decided to visit her in Santa Fe.

"I knew that he had become more interested in religion as he had gotten older. When we knew he was coming here, I said to Jody, 'Quick, where's the Synagogue?' So we went. It was small and I felt we knew almost everybody there, mostly people in business. Jody knew them because she'd been here a long time. Back then, most of the Plaza was owned by Jewish merchants who had their stores there. So when my father came to town, we just went around the Plaza and he got to visit with all the people and then that night we went to services and the same people were there. I realized it was a good thing. It wasn't a business decision, although we were in business at the time, but I liked the community. They were very welcoming. And Jody, who had been raised in Christian Science but had long since left that, decided she would like to convert. She took a year's course and I took it with her because I thought it would be good for me. I had realized that I really didn't have a good enough background to fully understand and participate. I only had the benefit of that period when I lived with my father. I had attended synagogue with his mother-in-law and had been with her many times on Friday nights when she lit the candles.

"I attended all the classes with Jody. She did better than I did because she's better in languages than I. I never learned any foreign language except French and I had a hard time with learning the Hebrew for the classes. At the end, after a year, the Rabbi has to certify that indeed, you know what you need to know. Also, in those days, the adult men of the congregation would also certify. We each had to write an essay on why we had chosen to join the faith. It was then sent to the Reformed Headquarters in Cincinnati. My response basically was that I needed to find out more about my background. After we were approved, there was a ceremony at the temple. We received a Hebrew name. Mine is Miriam Ruth bat Ephraim. Bat Ephraim means "daughter of Frank." From then on, I felt "legal." Before it had all been so vague. I'd really never had the resources to trace my ancestry back to Europe, so my grandmother's word that her mother was Jewish had been the only basis for thinking of myself as Jewish. I had always been fascinated by religion, but I never felt I had to be part of an organized religion. But I realized that I did find it satisfying to take part.

"At the time the only temple in Santa Fe was Temple Beth Shalom. It was in a small building where forty people at Friday services was a crowd. Jody and I were among the youngest of the adults. We became very active. I was on the Temple Board for several years and Jody was the second woman to be Temple President.

Her father's visit had not only returned him to Marcia's life, it had also catalyzed a new dimension to her life and Jody's. Family increased and their community broadened. Even after her father's death in 1972, their membership in their congregation remained strong for many years. And even though now in their later years, they no longer regularly attend services, they remain committed to the value of the religious community for the support that it offers to many others.

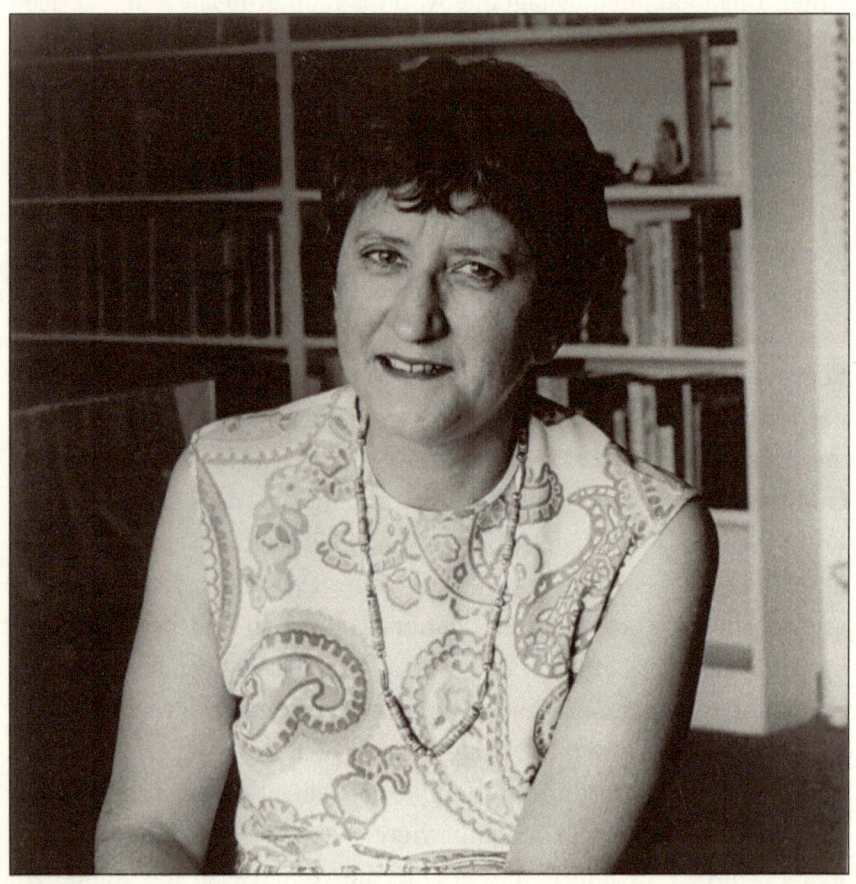

Marcia, 1970

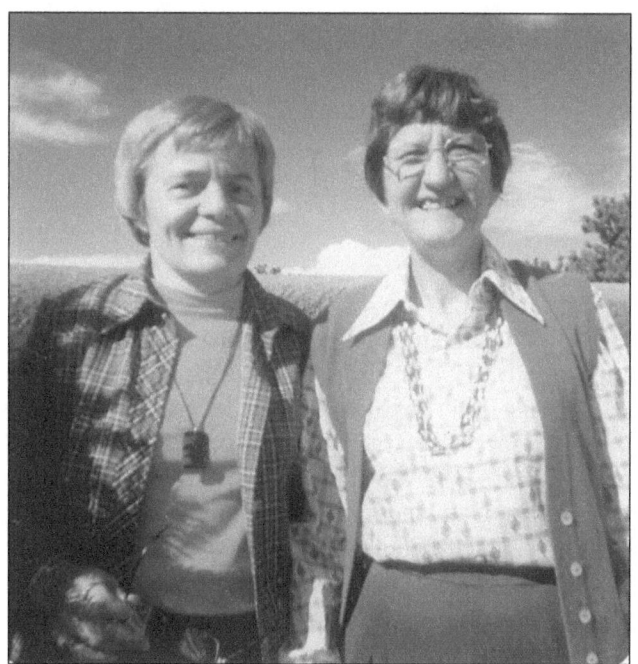

Allene Schnaitter and Marcia, 1972

Leaving Santa Fe

Wisdom in Greek was Sophia, as in our word "philoso-phy," love of wisdom. Sophia had a most practical mean-ing, referring originally to the crafts of handling things, especially to the helmsman who steers the boat. The wise one steers well; the wisdom of the helmsman shows in the art of making minor adjustments in accord with the acci-dents of water, wind, and weight. The daimon teaches this wisdom by constant appraisals of events that seem to pull you off course. Hillman, J., *The Soul's Code*, p. 206

The summer of 1976 marked a major change in Marcia's life. That was when John Reardon and Jim Smith broached an issue that involved them all. The subject of Sunstone's financial health had become a matter of concern. Although the publication list continued to grow and both she and Jody were fully occupied with creating and marketing the company's products, the investors proposed a change of leadership. The problem was financial. Debts had been mounting. The company was undercapitalized from the outset and John Reardon, as a principal stockholder, owning 51%, proposed that he buy out the founders' interest in the company. Jim Smith, although he would have preferred staying in New York and his job in advertising with New York Telephone, was to take over operations. His mission was to turn the operation to a profit in order to improve the company's financial picture and its possibility of surviving.

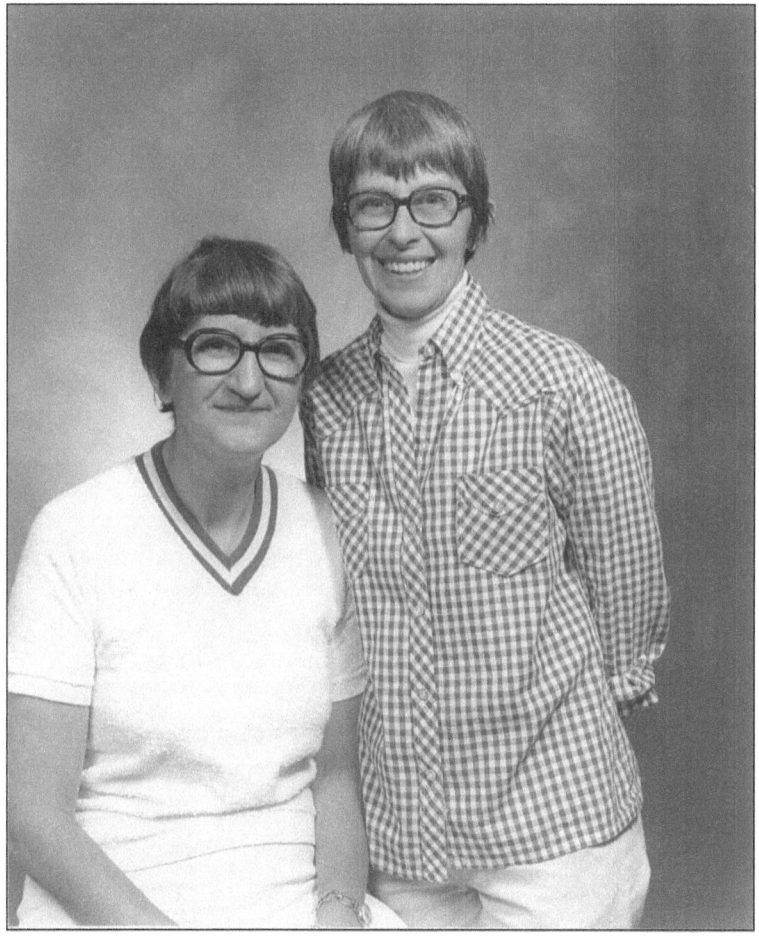

Marcia and Jody Ellis, 1974

"Both of them were just blown away. They had no hint that this was coming," recalled Marcia and Jody's friend Judith Armstrong. Although Marcia was asked to continue to work for the company, she and Jody decided to leave Santa Fe. One major consideration for Marcia was that she believed she could teach in college and that she could find an opportunity to do that in Missouri. Her previous experience in collegiate settings had encouraged her fascination with both the academic environment and the possibilities of teaching. In 1977, they moved to Springfield, Missouri.

Marcia wrote a poem, published in *Postcard Views and Other Souvenirs* titled "The Cast Iron Butterfly." It was published in 1973, so could not have been in response to the move that followed their choice to leave Santa Fe. But, it conveys a sense of loss and dismay that the move must have evoked.

> Moving again
> shelves nearly stripped
> bare
> like poorly picked bones;
> books, hunked flesh
> hanging to edges
> accenting the emptiness
> of unlived rooms.
> Most books are packed
> neat rows in marked cartons
> for the moment dead
> gone from touch and other senses.
> It takes time to pack books,
> I read every third one
> pieces of paragraphs
> inhaling the words
> feeling the text in my pores

remembering other occasions.
Some books, very few
will be left like broken toys
in the deserted playroom
of a yesterday mansion.
Yes, I must move
nomadized by events
computer decreed.
Dishes wrapped and ready
For unfolding
archaeologist, I will discover
my china in a new setting.
No chairs left free
I stand at curtainless window
balance a paper cup of coffee;
consider life, life today
instant coffee, instant love, instant death
I wait
look down at the street
I had meant to walk there
more slowly, more often
I look at my watch, no time now,
the van will be coming
and as a refugee
I must follow my possessions
down the stairs, across town
across this tired land.
Steam clouds my eyes
the coffee burns;
I taste all good-byes.
The van turns the corner
I turn away
my heart, a cast iron butterfly.

Judith Armstrong is a friend whom Marcia first met when they were both at the libraries at the University of Missouri in Columbia. In 1965, Armstrong had moved to Springfield to work at the library at the University of Southwest Missouri. Through the connection with Ms. Armstrong, Marcia and Jody found work in Springfield. Marcia had her first opportunity to teach formal courses. She taught English classes at both Drury College and at University of Southwest Missouri. She also worked at the Springfield Public Library and at the Drury College Library.

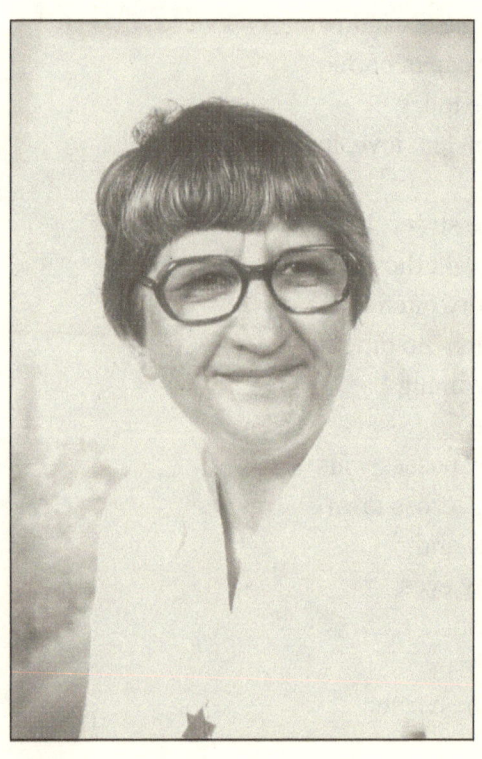

Marcia, 1974

She enjoyed the experience at the front of the classroom. "I love teaching. Anyone who knows me will tell you that I've never entered an auditorium or a lecture hall where I didn't want to be up front, doing the lecture," Marcia said. "Earlier when I was in college, I would have loved to go on and become a professor. But, in all the years I was there, I had only one woman professor. She taught astronomy and she had never advanced beyond the lower ranks. She was a wonderful teacher but she was a curiosity. When I was at the law school, we had only a handful of women students and not one woman law professor. So, the only option that seemed reasonable to me was to continue as a librarian."

In about 1975 Marcia had begun to explore other forms of creative expression. She considered the print-making that she had done earlier. Rather than return to that process that had caused physical problems with her hands, she decided to try painting. She experimented with different approaches to use of color and different subjects. Her work at Sunstone precluded her investing a large amount of her time in developing her interest, however. She never doubted her ability as a librarian, nor as a writer, particularly as a poet. But as she began as a painter, she didn't have that same degree of confidence. She had no formal training to guide her. The change of routine that the move to Missouri offered provided the time to begin to develop the new skills.

Jody had been painting miniatures for several years and was successful at exhibiting and selling them. But after Marcia began to work seriously at art, Jody saw that Marcia was the better artist and the one who should concentrate on painting. Marcia disagreed about who was the better artist, but agreed to Jody's idea, primarily because Jody wanted to devote herself to a different artistic interest. She intended to pursue her love of music more seriously by becoming a cellist. Both have succeeded admirably with the new forms of art they chose.

Factories were a favorite subject for Marcia as she focused on developing as an artist. She had a lifelong interest in architecture and a fondness for those buildings that housed enterprises so important in the cities where she had spent her early years. Later she began to add humans to her paintings, although she hesitated because she felt hers did not seem lifelike. "I still have trouble with hands and feet," she said.

As her confidence in her ability grew, she identified another special interest that she felt could be best expressed through her art. Scenes from life in the 1930s were her forte. She had observed all of those scenes of a way of life that had all but vanished. She now had a focus and her skills were increasing with each new painting.

By 1980, the heat and humidity in Missouri were more than Marcia wanted to tolerate. And Jody only felt at home in Santa Fe. So, they decided to move back West. Marcia returned with new skills and interests in painting that would before long, as she described it, "just take over" in a way that even her writing had never done. She was not yet comfortable calling herself a painter, but she knew that depicting the scenes of her favorite period in this country's history was an important part of who she was.

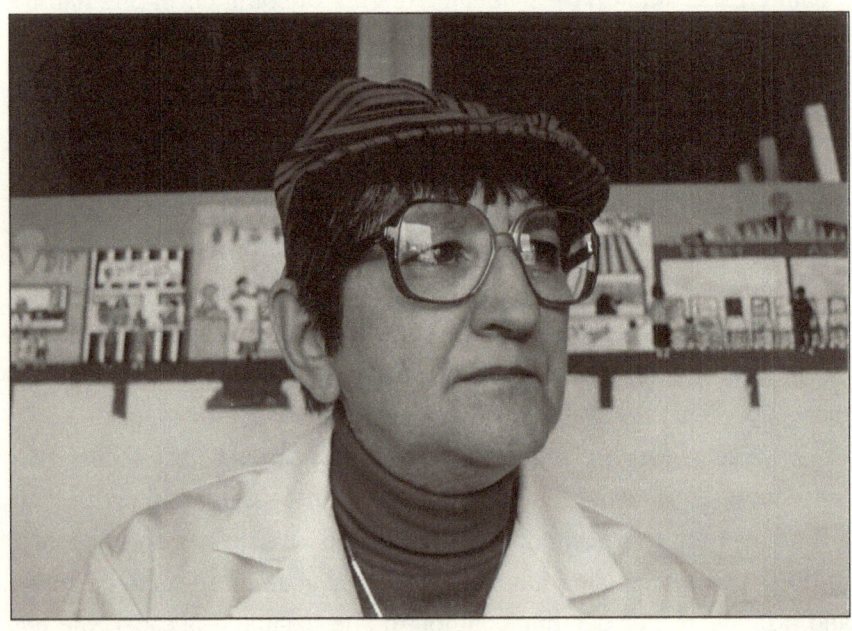

Marcia In Front of Painting (*Orman Beach*), 1982

A Writer Who Paints or a Painter Who Writes Poetry

The pull of purpose comes with force; you may feel full of purpose. But just what it is and how to get there remains undetermined. The telos may even be double or triple and confused about whether to sing or dance; write or paint. Purpose does not usually appear as a clearly framed goal, but more as a troubling, unclear urge coupled with a sense of indubitable importance. Hillman, J., *The Soul's Code*, p. 197

Naïve art is a broad term that describes the work of people who have had no formal training in art or are self-taught. Many other descriptions are applied to the work of naïve artists based on the primary medium that is used (for example, painting, sculpture, constructions with found materials); the subject matter (memory, religious subjects, current events); or the relationship of the art to more classical and formal artistic forms (outsider art, raw art, brut art). Marcia Muth's art clearly fits the general category of naïve art because she had no formal instruction in art.

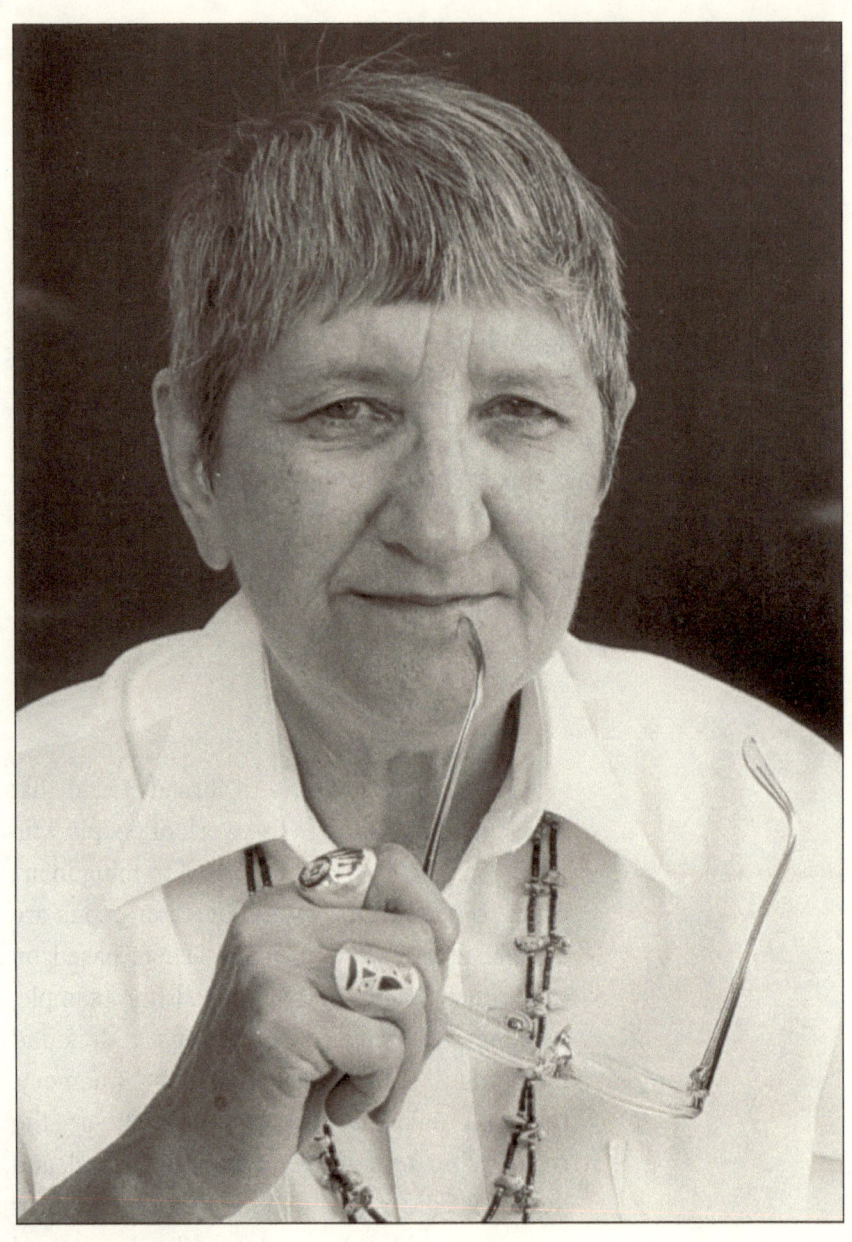

Marcia, 1992

Another category that commonly describes the work of untutored artists is folk art. This too is less than specific in that all manner of work can be viewed as folk art so long as the work reflects a lack of concern with elaborate composition and sophisticated organization more typical of classical forms of art. As a result, folk art has a type of simplicity and imagination and often expresses something of the lives of "common people." Richard Guy Wilson, in the article "Contemporary American Folk Art: Charming Junk or Art with a Capital A?" mentions that the 1970s and 1980s were a period of increased interest in folk art, perhaps because of cultural changes in the United States including some in academia that included a new focus on the life of common persons and away from the study of great men.

One category of folk art is memory paintings. The classification is related to the subject matter of the paintings—recollections of the painter of scenes from his or her life. These works are most often of rural scenes and often of the South or of Appalachian scenes, based on the background of the artist.

In Marcia's case, the term naïve art was accurate because she was self-taught. More specifically, her paintings of recollections of the era of the 1930s, of common people's lives situated her in the realm of folk art. Her paintings are memory paintings, but unlike most of the earlier memory painters such as Grandma Moses, she did not paint rural scenes from the 19th and early 20th centuries. And her scenes were urban, not rural. But, not surprisingly, she was less concerned about the classification of her work than about what she viewed as creating visual history.

As she painted, her confidence in her skill grew. She began to sell her work, but only enough to buy a bit more than supplies. The skills in which she had confidence, her ability as a librarian, provided the day job that was necessary to help meet living expenses. When they returned to Santa Fe, she began working at the Museum of New Mexico's History Library.

Promise of a shortened work week that would allow more time for her art enticed Marcia to return to work at Sunstone. "John and Jim asked me to come back, said they needed me. It was true that I had always been good with public relations and I also did editing. Jim really wanted me back. They said that they would pay me what I was making at the Museum and I could have Saturday, Sunday and Monday off to work on my art. By that time John had even bought some of my paintings. So, I went back," she said.

Marcia and Jody's prior social relationship with Smith and Reardon gradually resumed. "John was an interesting person. He was accustomed to being a star. All of us were satellites to that star even if we didn't realize it. It was my only experience with knowing someone like that. It was only later looking back that I realized how it was. He'd say, 'We'll do this.' And that's what we'd do. We revolved around him. At one time not too long before he died in 1988 he was offered a position as Chair of the Voice Department at some college in California. He decided that we'd all move out to California with him. If it had ever come to that, Jody and I wouldn't have gone," Marcia said.

Although painting consumed much of her interest during the 1980s, Marcia did not completely abandon writing. Four non-poetry books that she wrote between 1983 and 1985 were published by Sunstone Press. Those were *Is It Safe To Drink The Water: A Guide To Santa Fe* (1983); *How to Paint and Sell Your Art* (1984); *Kachinas: A Selected Bibliography* (1984); and *Writing and Selling Poetry, Fiction, Articles, Plays and Local History* (1985). *Thin Ice and Other Poems* (1987) demonstrated that poetry had not been entirely supplanted by painting as a medium of her expression. Several of the poems in that volume had appeared in periodicals such as *American Bard, Green World, Arizona Quarterly* and *New Lantern Club Review*. "A Passion For Words" included in *Thin Ice* reflects a sense of her creative self that, at least at that time, still had a strong verbal element.

I write poems secretly
At work
Riding in the car
In waiting rooms
I am besieged by words
They hang in the air
Butterflies
I pin them to my paper

By 1985 Marcia had begun to feel that she was accomplished enough to actually think of herself as a painter. One of her first appearance in a traveling show came in 1987, when she was included in "The Magic of Naïve." The paintings toured several museums and galleries in Indiana, Illinois, and Wisconsin. Her first solo show was in 1985 at the Yolanda Gallery of Naïve Art in Chicago. Several other group exhibits followed in the next ten years as did four other solo shows. By the late 1990s her work had become a part of public collections at the Museum of Fine Art in Santa Fe, New Mexico; the Museum of Naïve Art, Paris, France; the Jewish Museum, New York City; the Art Museum of Southeast Texas, Beaumont, Texas; and the Albuquerque Museum.

She had adapted to working at Sunstone on the four day schedule and spending the rest of her days painting. She began taking commissions for her work. Many who have become collectors of Marcia Muth were as interested in the era that she paints as in her style. Their interest translated to frequent commission work because Marcia will add touches to the details of a painting to personalize it for the patron. Some have asked for a particular business that is in their family to be represented in the work. Others described an event, such as a family reunion, that they wanted translated to her 1930s perspective.

Marcia also began teaching with the Santa Fe branch of the Elderhostel program. Elderhostel is designed to combine travel and education for older learners. Founded in 1975, the program has a variety of sites on several continents where students learn about topics ranging from local history to the environment to arts and culture. Whenever possible the students are housed on a local college campus and combine structured classes and tours with free time for exploring the local scene. Santa Fe is one of Elderhostel's most popular destinations.

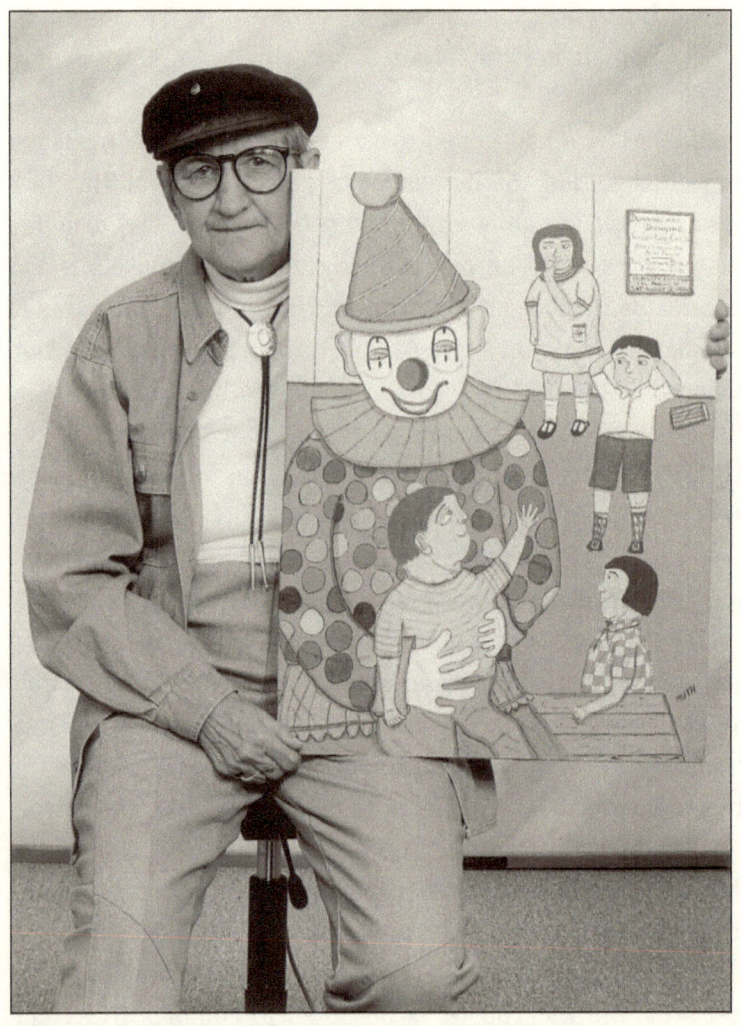

Marcia With Painting (*Rudi the Clown*)**, 1995**

Marcia explained how she became a part of the Elderhostel faculty. "While Jody and I were living in Springfield I noticed an ad in the classifieds from a woman who was opening an art gallery, Mary Anne Fellows. I contacted her and she came and looked at our work, both mine and Jody's miniatures. She liked what she saw and said she wanted us in her gallery. We got acquainted with her and her husband. She was also a singer. He mentioned that at one time he'd lived in New Mexico and would love to return. Then after we were back here in Santa Fe we met the founder and director of the Desert Chorale. He was looking for singers. So we wrote Mary Anne to suggest she audition. She did and was hired. Her husband sold his floor covering factory and they moved here. She sang with the Chorale but after a while she took a job with the College of Santa Fe as coordinator of the local Elderhostel.

"One day she called and said a person who was to lecture that evening couldn't be there. Could I fill in? She said I could talk about the literature of the area, bring samples. So after that she asked if I wanted to teach regularly. Of course I did because I love to teach and I could combine two of my favorite topics, art and the Santa Fe area."

Comments from some former Elderhostel students explain their response to Marcia and to her art. "She's upbeat, enthusiastic, and whimsical," said Mary Jean Kerr. "I have a painting I commissioned that hangs in my home. People marvel at it because my grandson's name is in the scene and it's such a pleasure to look at. I also have another piece in black and white—*Elm City Ballet.* I think her work is better than Grandma Moses."

Mary Lou Colgin said, "Knowing Marcia has enriched my life. It's wonderful to meet people of her age who are doing exciting things." She described Marcia as forthright and creative. She also said, "I like her primitive style of painting. It's very consistent; you know what to expect. It's just a charming 'Marcia style' that catches the spirit of the place she paints."

"We continue to write one another every few months, just

staying in touch. And we've visited Marcia and Jody three or four times when we've been in the area since we met at Elderhostel in two thousand. Her lectures enlarged my knowledge of Southwestern Art and helped me become aware of other local artists," Ginny Ott said. She and her husband Ted own six pieces of Marcia's art, some of which they commissioned.

Marcia enjoyed the performance aspect of teaching. She interlaced facts and concepts about art and the Southwest with anecdotes about some of the artists she had known. She was quick to poke a bit of fun at herself, too. "I'm still not very good at self-promotion. I used to tell my Elderhostel students that when I first started painting I kept my work a secret. I said, 'You'd think I was doing pornography.' If only I had been doing pornography, I'd be rich and famous," she said.

This new focus, beyond literary activity, brought a widening of her network of contacts. Marcia had practiced networking before the term came into vogue. Just as she had with friends and professional acquaintances from her prior activities, she maintained contact with her new art-related friends and acquaintances by writing letters and by sending personalized holiday greetings, usually containing poetry. When any of those individuals traveled to the Southwest, they were invited to visit. Many of the Elderhostel students became part of her web of contacts as did others to whom she sold her art.

Others beyond her Elderhostel students also learned of Marcia's work. Betty Carol Sellen attended an event sponsored by the Folk Art Explorer Club through the American Folk Art Museum in New York City. Ms. Sellen's interests in twentieth century American folk, self taught, and outsider art have been the source for several books she has written on those subjects. "When I first met her, she and Jody came to the Eldorado Hotel to pick me up. There were both so small and perfect and were wearing matching hats," she said. She went to visit at their home to see Marcia's studio and stayed for a couple of hours. After that she visited every year or two for several years. To her Marcia is more than an acquaintance; she's a friend. Ms. Sellen liked Marcia's art very much, particularly what she saw of Marcia's images of the Jewish community recalled from her youth. "She's a very creative person, full of life and intensely interested in everything. Besides Marcia's art, I remember a poem of hers that really got to me," she said. That poem was "Hall of the American Indian—Third Floor, North Wing."

Ms. Sellen said she displays Marcia's art in each of her two homes. "I can look at them a lot and often and I find something new each time. I'm always amused that the faces she paints all look alike and I love her use of color."

Florence and Jules Laffal were among the first to visit Marcia in Santa Fe because of her art. One of the subscribers to the newsletter they published, *Folk Art Finder,* suggested that they contact her as they were interested in introducing their readers to unknown artists. In 1981 they were planning a trip west so they arranged to meet with Marcia during that trip.

"We were interested in the fact that Marcia was a memory painter, but not of the usual kind. Normally we think of memory painters, such as Grandma Moses, painting rural scenes remembered from the past. Marcia's memories of her years in Indiana were quite different. We published an article about her and her work. She was very grateful to us because we were the first to do that. We became owners of two of her paintings and were pleased to be her discoverers."

After beginning work with Elderhostel around 1988, Marcia's schedule of work began to compress her time for art. So Marcia reevaluated. "By then, it had just taken over," she said, speaking of her art. And painting had also overshadowed poetry as her creative interest. The day job was an unnecessary interference in her "real work." She decided to retire from Sunstone Press. "They were well organized and after John died in 1988, I didn't feel obligated to continue there. So I retired. After that we didn't have much contact with Jim. Occasionally I would stop in the offices because they still had my books and I was friendly with Brenda who was Jim's assistant," she said.

The retirement and subsequent change in contact with Jim Smith and with Sunstone Press was less a single event than the eventual result of Marcia's emerging change of focus. Now she was an artist and her primary energies were channeled into making art and teaching about it. She wrote poems when they came to her, but she did not search for them. She did not lose her love of words, but she had gained an overpowering affection for creating visual history—new purpose.

Friends and Obligations

The Platonic myth of growing down . . . says the soul
descends in four modes—via the body, the parents, the place,
and circumstances. The four ways can be instructions for
completing the image you brought with you on arrival. First,
your body. Growing down means giving in to the sag of gravity
that accompanies aging . . . Second, admitting yourself to
be one among your people and a member of the family tree,
including its twisted and rotten branches. Third, living in a
place that suits your soul and that ties you down with duties
and customs. Last, giving back what circumstance gave you
by means of gestures that declare your full attachment to this
world. Hillman, J., *The Soul's Code*, p. 62

I
f, as Hillman writes the myth, the soul
descends and does so in part by means
of "being one among your people and
a member of your family tree, including its
twisted and rotten branches . . . and living in a
place that suits your soul and that ties you down
with duties and customs . . . ." Marcia Muth's
soul has been on that journey.

Her immediate family dwindled to
one by the 1980s, her Aunt Doris. Rather than
continue the family tradition of "out of sight,
out of mind," Marcia stayed in regular contact

with Doris Bernhardt. "Even after she realized there was no chance it would ever happen, Auntie continued hoping that I would find some nice man to marry. But she did like Jody and she knew we were happy," she said.

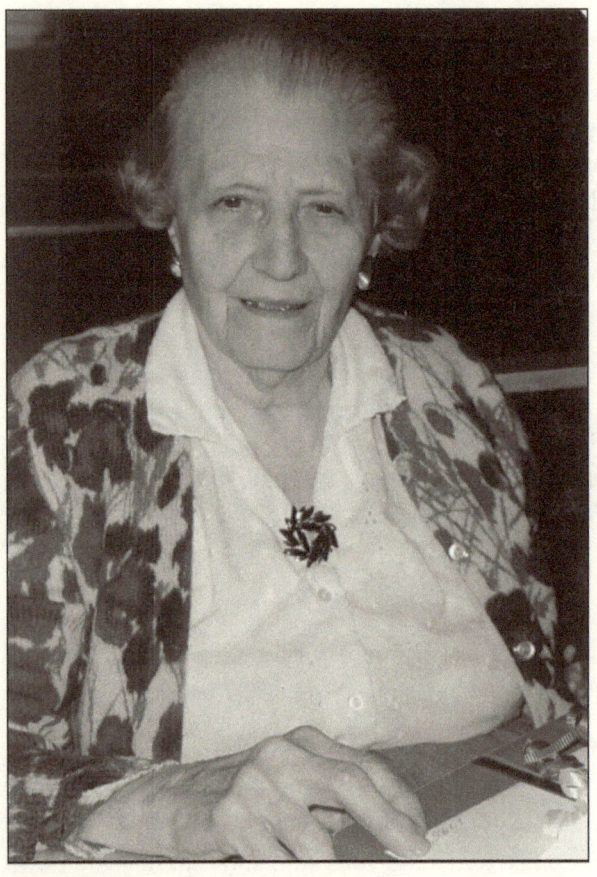

Doris Bernhardt, Age 90, 1995

Doris and her husband Lee had no children and as Marcia recalled them, had never seemed particularly happy together. Describing Lee after World War II when he had traveled frequently to Boston for his work, Marcia said, "He got more and more withdrawn. He read a lot. After he retired from General Electric, he taught at a technical college and that seemed to revive him for a while. I heard him say once when someone asked about something my aunt had said, 'I don't know. I haven't heard a word she said in twenty years.' He had adjusted to their life—he completely removed himself. And she never seemed to notice, except when he got sick. Then she put him in a nursing home. He died in April, nineteen eighty-one."

Marcia and her Aunt Doris maintained frequent contact by telephone and letters. "She was never one to express much emotion. We usually talked about ordinary things, not about feelings. But I will say that she always seemed genuinely interested in me and my life. She asked details such as what we served for a particular dinner party or what I wore to an event or who we met at some occasion. That made me feel good.

"She had always given names to objects in her house and when she was older and had to use a walker, she named it 'Buster.' Sometimes, 'Buster' would say hello to me on the phone. He had a voice that was different from Auntie's. One time she said, 'Buster wants to talk to you.' So when Buster spoke, after we said our hellos, he said, 'You know, Mrs. B. really loves you.' I told 'him' I knew. That was the only time she ever said she loved me.

"At one time we invited her to come out and live here, but she chose not to because all of her friends were there. She lived her last months in a nursing home and she mentioned often that she was concerned that she was running out of money."

Marcia was surprised when her aunt died in June, 2002, at the age of 96, that she actually was not destitute. "She made a point in her will—no service, immediate burial. They called me from the funeral home and asked if I wanted to do something, some sort of service. I said, 'No, those were her wishes. All her friends are dead or in a nursing home and I haven't lived there since nineteen forty-three.'

"Her obituary said she was a Presbyterian. She hadn't been to church in years, but that church had this arrangement for senior citizens at one time where they would call and check on them. She appreciated that so she left money to the church flower fund. They'd sent her flowers several times. She also left money to the local humane society. She left some money to me which was a most welcome surprise because it has made life a little more comfortable for me and Jody. We don't have to be quite so concerned if we have an unexpected repair or an emergency."

The memory painter and Jody Ellis have made a home and a life that expresses their individual and mutual interests and welcomes friends and visitors. One friend, Gail Kaplan, commented, "It's like a perpetual salon at their house."

Sasha, the dog, and Chuckie, the cat, share with them a comfortable house in a quiet Santa Fe neighborhood. The yard is a combination of xeriscape and plastic gardening. And, although the plastic flamingos and assorted 'flowers' are interesting, it's the interior that demonstrates the blending of two complementary personalities.

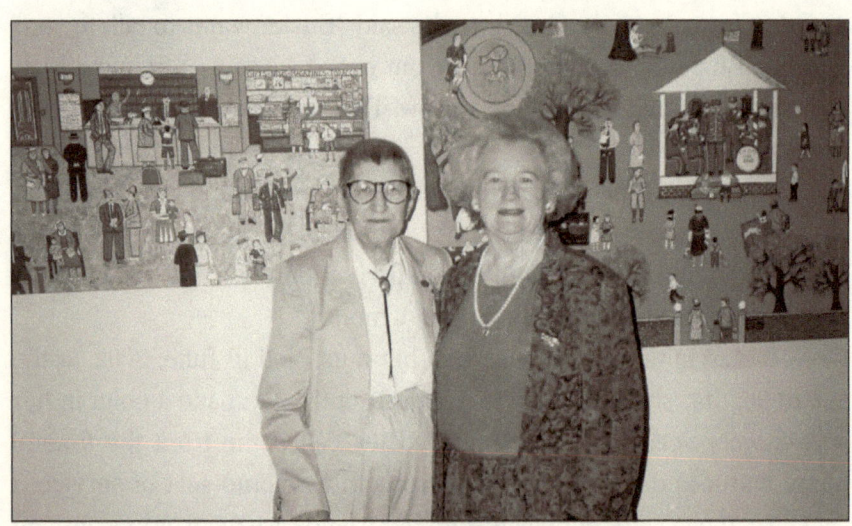

Marcia and Alice King at Exhibit in Governor's Gallery, Santa Fe, 1994

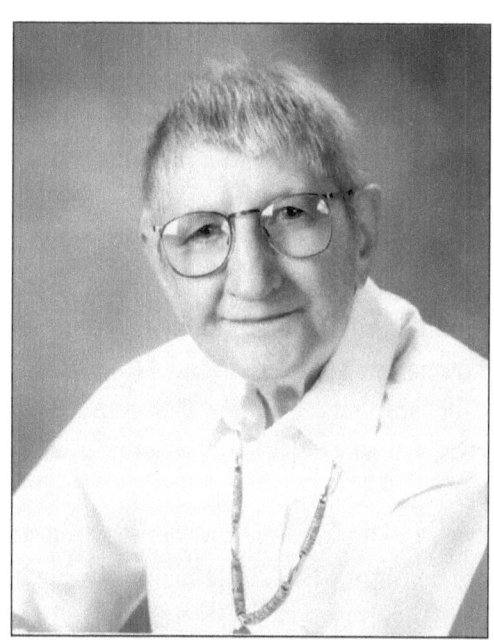

Marcia, 1997

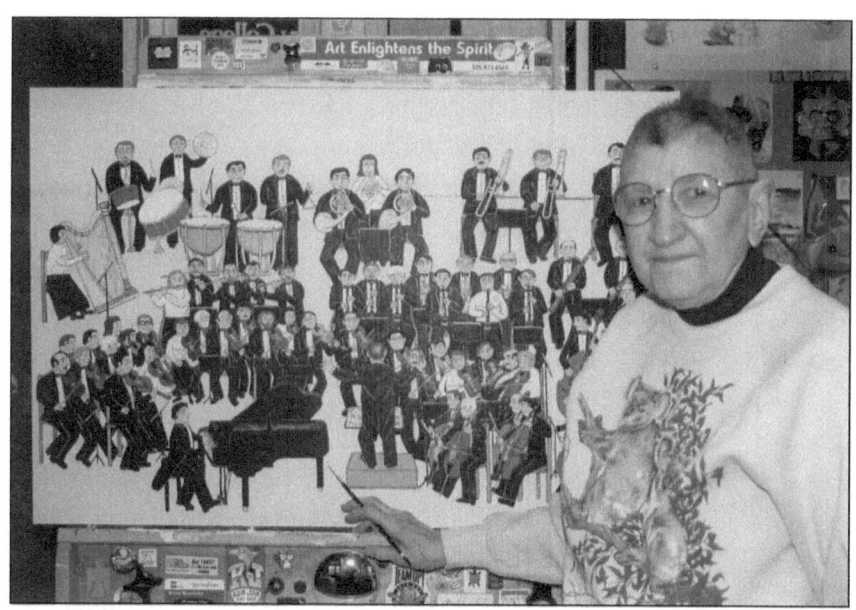

Marcia With Painting (*Piano Concerto*)**, 2000**

Marcia's studio contains three easels each with a painting in progress, at any moment. Her collection of art books competes for space with fanciful items such as a waterless aquarium that contains painted paper fish and a plastic deep sea diver. She paints there every day except Sunday. She explained, "I have to catch up on other things at least once a week."

Jody's music studio occupies the next room, accessible from both the kitchen and the living room. The cheery greeting with which Marcia answers the phone, "Ellis Studio," conveys the fact that Jody's cello students and her Community Orchestra involvement create a steady flow of visitors. The studio welcomes musicians of a variety of ages.

The kitchen and dining area are utilitarian. The uses include meals, nightly Boggle games, and a display of tiny toy trucks and cars that is changed each week. Several of Jody's miniature paintings from years ago decorate the walls. The refrigerator and microwave are labeled with their respective names (Francine and Jack) as are the television (Rex) and several other items. The weekly agenda of the Prairie Dogettes, International may be found here on the weekend. The two-person club, comprising members Marcia and Jody, heralds its weekend of social and cultural activities with a written agenda. Marcia prepares the docket chronicling company meals, visitors, and topics for discussion or focus of activities.

The small living room contains Rex, primarily used for viewing C-Span, news, documentaries and arts programs. Marcia's regular two-newspaper daily reading habit results in a cache of overflow newsprint. The walls abound with her art, all colorful, each containing what one friend appreciates most about her paintings. "There's always something in each one of them that's a little off—a crooked seam, a napkin on the floor, a spill," Gail Kaplan said.

Two bedrooms, two baths, and an office complete the home. It all reflects the eclectic owners. Nothing here is lavish. The home does not say "Celebrity Santa Fe." It says comfortable and artistic. And nothing other than Marcia's portable oxygen tank, "Buster, Jr.," suggests age or infirmity. At 88, Marcia said, "We live each day." Jody added, "Never forget to be a child. Always find time to play." Those words form a credo for them, it seems.

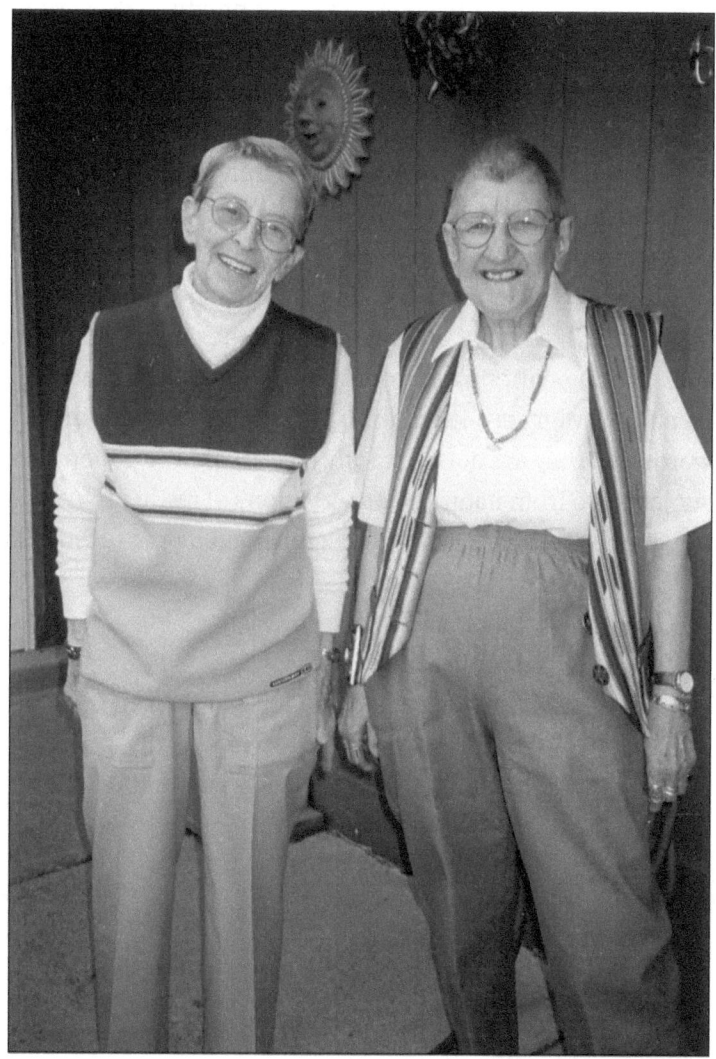

Jody Ellis and Marcia, 2000

"Buster, Jr." is the only evidence that Marcia's lungs require assistance to compensate for Santa Fe's high altitude. She won't dwell on a discussion of the exact nature of her lungs' weakness although a lifelong history of pulmonary problems such as bronchitis suggest it's chronic. Accepting medical advice in 2006 to use the oxygen daily was not easy for her—the fifty-foot tube is something of a leash—but she did agree that it has improved her ability to do her work. Another ailment diagnosed years ago, lupus erythematosus, has limited her time outdoors because sun exposure exacerbates the disease. "I used to walk twice every day in all kinds of weather. I observed nature and that was a source of ideas for poems. Now, I rely on my imagination because I've had to stay indoors more. *Words and Images*, published in 2004, contains several poems that demonstrate that her imagination continues to provide vivid imagery of the nature she must now observe less frequently. That book combines drawings, poems, and some narrative. The drawings offer a different view of this artist's memory than do her paintings. Many are fanciful; all fit thematically with the accompanying words, but they are not tied to any particular time period. More often, the subjects are from nature or observations of life in progress. An example is a drawing of a large raven, accompanied by the poem, "Raven's Call."

I look into the trees
For direction
A raven calls out to me
Guide or trickster?
I am uncertain about his advice
His invitation
To follow him down the trail
Into the woods
And when I stop, hesitating
He flies away
His last calls echo to the sky
Blessing or curse?

The major concern that Marcia's changing physical health has produced is not for herself. "For a while I felt guilty that I couldn't do as much of the housework and cooking and such. But Jody told me not to be concerned, that I should do my work—that's what's important. She says she likes to take care of me. So I decided to get over feeling that way."

"Like family" was the label several chose when asked to describe their relationship with Marcia Muth. Sondra Everhart, who first met Marcia about 13 years ago, once said, "I think Marcia and I are a bit similar in that we both are a bit shy, but warm." Describing Marcia's way of dealing with adversity, she said, "She's practical. She just takes the view that life gets tough sometimes. You don't let it stop you. Marcia could have coined the phrase 'Suck it up.'"

Roslyn Eisenberg lives about four blocks from Marcia and Jody. She too thinks of Marcia as family. For years she has enjoyed visiting with Marcia in her studio and chatting as she watches her paint. "She's interested in so many things. And things she sees and does go into her art and her writing. An example is the fish. We've gone several times to the aquarium. She's absolutely enchanted by the fish—has written about the fish and painted *Drollites Go To The Aquarium* and some beautiful imaginary fish," she said.

The Drollites are imaginary beings, not found in nature. But they definitely have unique and recognizable characteristics found in other species. Their heads have dog-like features and long erect ears. Their bodies, or maybe it's their tribal costume, are long and shapeless. There are two three-toed feet and two hands (or paws?) that each have three fingers which are apparently opposable; they often hold implements or ice cream cones or umbrellas.

The Drollite drawings, several of which are included in *Words and Images*, show them in a variety of activities. They appear to be very social and active. They are members of orchestras; they dance; they walk in the rain; and they always smile. One of the youngsters has a dog. It's said by their inventor that they love ice cream.

These fanciful creatures are quite different from Marcia Muth's memory paintings. But an underlying similarity is the smile that they bring to the viewer. Their species name, Drollite, begins an etymologic chain: *droll*—amusingly odd, whimsical; *whimsical*—playful, capricious; *capricious*—playful, odd, fantastic, unusual. All the links in that chain are equally apt for both the drawings and the artist.

"Marcia inspires me. She's affected my art through our discussions and in other ways. I think of her as a best friend, a mentor. She and Jody are the mothers I never had," Marilyn Fisher said. She usually sees Marcia about once a week, just to talk about art, books, politics, or other subjects. She met Marcia through her husband Willard Chilcott who was one of the first members of the Santa Fe Community Orchestra, a group that Jody helped found in 1983. He and Marilyn also have dinner with Marcia and Jody about once a month. Willard said, "I think of them as inseparable. Jody is the more romantic and Marcia is the leavening agent."

Another member of the family that Marcia has grown into is Jim Smith. "I think of him as a brother." She and Jim saw one another only occasionally after her retirement from Sunstone.

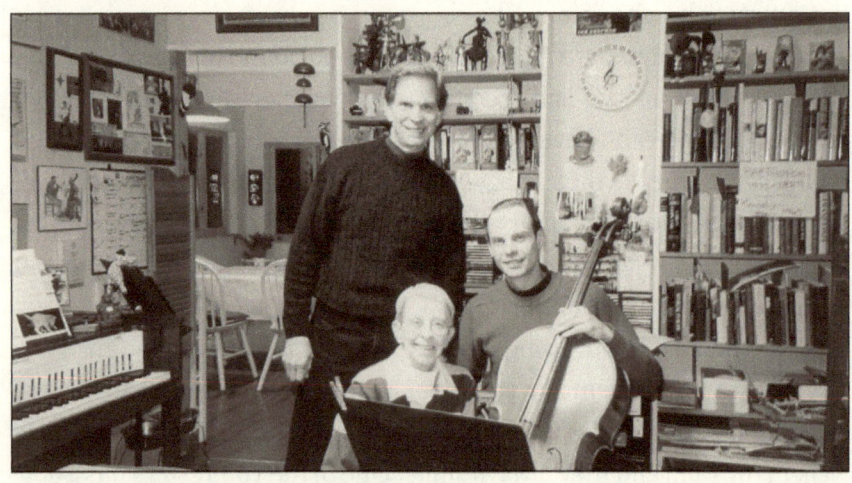

Jim Smith, Jody Ellis, and Carl Condit, 2002

"Then, sort of out of the blue, in about two thousand, he called and asked if Jody might give cello lessons to a friend of his. He said the friend wanted to brush up on his technique and learn more. After he asked what she charged and when there could be a lesson, he said he'd see me then. A few days later Carl Condit came for the lesson and Jim came with him. While Carl had his lesson, Jim and I sat on the couch and talked—it was originally Jim and John's couch, I recalled.

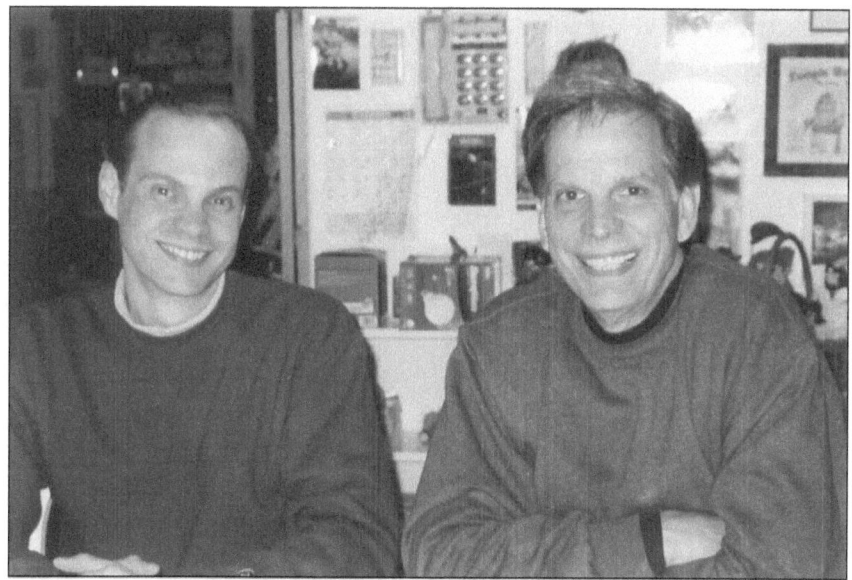

Carl Condit and Jim Smith

"When the lesson was finished, they left, saying we'd all get together again. And we did. Now they come almost every Friday night for dinner and we have lunch on Wednesdays. Sometimes they come by on the weekend too.

"I do consider Jim as a brother. I enjoy his company and I've asked his advice in things I'm doing. For example, I took his recommendation for the attorney that I used for Allene's business. Jim and Carl have become our family members. They look after us, help us with household projects and the yard."

Jim's view of Marcia reflects hers. His encouragement for her art is strong. "He told me I should charge more for my paintings," she said. He was also a strong factor in encouraging Marcia to develop her recent book, *A World Set Apart: Memory Paintings*, published by Sunstone in 2007. The book highlights her art with a series of excellent color photographs of paintings and with Marcia's narrative describing the scenes. He also encouraged her to develop *"Words and Images,"* published in 2004.

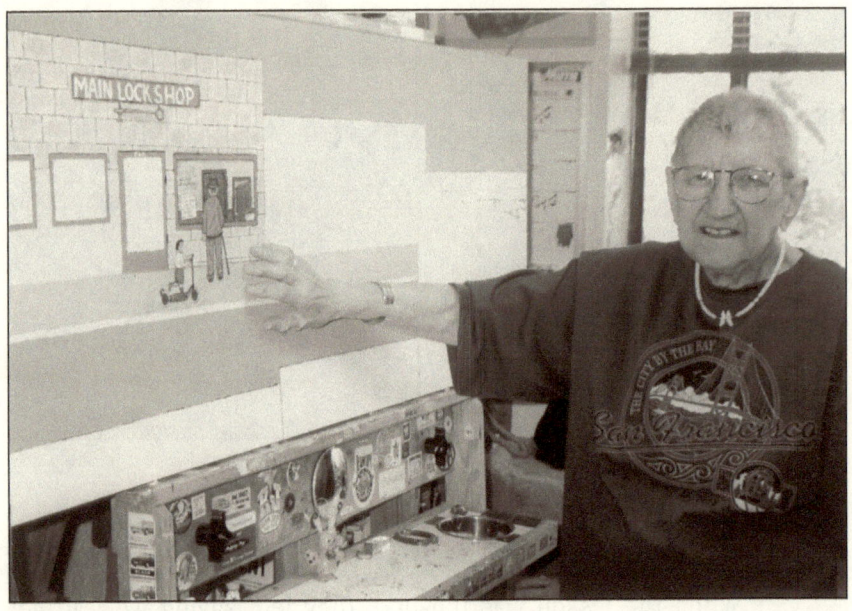

Marcia in Studio, 2002

Besides her work, the painting she loves and does daily and the family of friends she has assembled, Marcia has "grown down" through working to meet another responsibility. For years, she managed the affairs of her friend and former partner Allene Schnaitter, who died in an Alzheimer's care facility in 2007.

"It's interesting about Allene. I've often wondered why she never took up with anyone else. Why did she move to Santa Fe when she retired? I think it was because she wanted to be near us. In a way she was horning in. She was just a friend, but when her mind began to go, she became a bit of a nuisance. She would come over and not want to go home; she wanted to move in.

"Maybe she was lonely. At the same time that she would imply she wanted to find someone, a little friend, she didn't go about trying to make friends in the best way. She was bossy when she was in her right mind. She would tell me I would end up on welfare. She had a lot more money than we had and in some ways she was generous. At the holidays she'd sometimes give me a thousand dollar check. And at one time she wanted to give me one of her rent houses. Tax-wise that wasn't suitable, but in her last years before she went to the nursing home, she was still capable and would bring me half the rent check from that house, saying it really ought to be mine.

"She was very fond of Jody. Because Jody was a nurse, anytime Allene had an ache or pain she would come and ask her what to do.

"Some years before, when she moved out to Santa Fe, she had designated me to have power of attorney and to be executor of her affairs, without telling me. She had brought by an envelope and just said to keep it, that it had important papers in it. I filed it without looking inside. It was only when she became ill and was clearly unable to make rational decisions that I remembered the envelope. I went out in the garage where it was filed and read it. I consulted a lawyer who said that since no one else had been named since that was written, the statement was still in effect. So, that made it a little easier to get her proper care."

Providing for Allene's care was not a simple matter of admitting her to a nursing facility. Marcia and Jody visited regularly to assure that her care was maintained and Marcia attended to Allene's business affairs including dealing with rental property and the inevitable details of tenants and upkeep.

"Over the years, Allene had been a staunch Democrat and somewhat of an activist for various causes. For some reason she had it in for big corporations, even though that's where her money was invested. When her mind began to go, she didn't want to pay her utility bills—didn't want the big company to get the money. Or she'd go and offer to pay them a hundred dollars, a portion of the bill.

"Eventually her family became concerned and asked her to move where they live in Ohio. She refused. She wanted to stay here. But she did begin to decline. Besides the other behavior that was difficult, physical things began to change. For example, she would seem to be unaware of where her legs were. Someone would have to move them for her or remind her to move them. We saw that happen at a Fourth of July party that we had here at home. We had put card tables here and there to serve the meal. Two of the tables were in the music room and she sat down at one of them. I noticed that her legs were not under the table. So I took her feet and placed them under the table.

"She also started to look like a bag lady. She had long liked the idea of appearing that way. Even years ago in Ann Arbor, she had told me she envied a woman on the campus who dressed like that and just wandered around, picking up things off the ground. Allene thought that was a wonderful way to live. So in a way, she began to live that out. I would tell her that her clothes were torn or she needed to bathe. She would say, 'Why?' At least after she was in the nursing facility, she was clean even though she was unaware of it.

"For some reason, even though she was always critical of me—I wasn't sharp enough about business; I didn't have big important jobs; I hadn't planned for the future—she was attached to me, then to us. But, I think that if she had been able, she'd be proud of Jody and me."

The sources of the possible pride that her friend might have felt could be many. Marcia Muth's soul has made a long journey; she's one among a family; she lives in a place that suits her soul. And if having plans, continuing obligations, and work in progress are any indications, she expects to continue that journey.

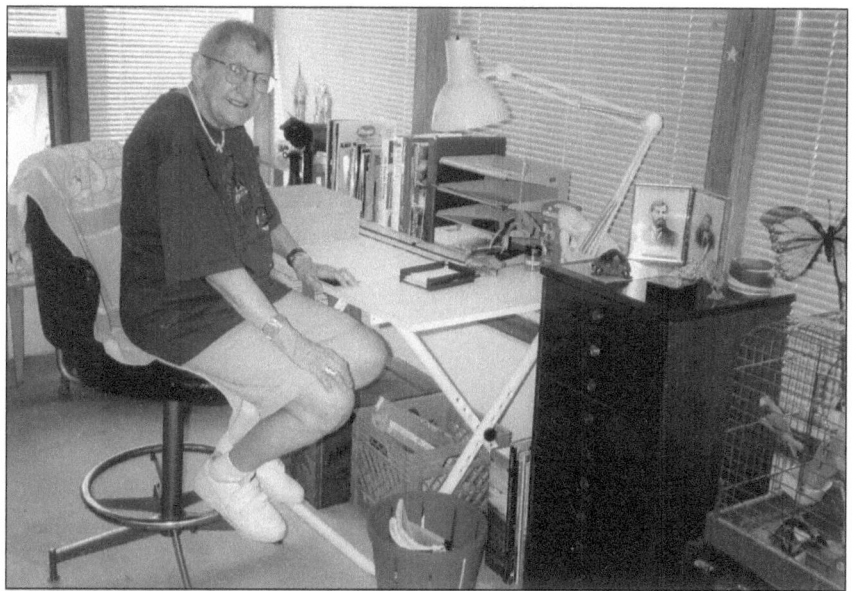

Marcia, 2002

Two Openings

> A calling may be postponed, avoided, intermittently missed. It may also possess one completely. Whatever; eventually it will out. It makes its claim. The daimon does not go away. Hillman, J., *The Soul's Code*, p. 8

"We're not, never have been activists. The only prejudice or discrimination I ever felt I experienced was as a Jew," Marcia said. She was explaining about the decision she and Jody made in 2005 to participate in the Santa Fe production of "The Out Monologues."

"The Out Monologues" is one aspect of the Life Monologues Project developed by Pamela Thompson beginning in 2000. She created the project from the belief "that subjects and audiences gain more when people tell their own stories. In recent years public appetite for the theater of truth and dramatized oral history has increased." Her conviction that the process of telling the personal stories could be a healing process grew from her own experiences after the death of her husband from cancer.

In comparison to other monologue theater such as "The Vagina Monologues," which is performed by actors, Thompson's project develops the stories of actual individuals, told by those persons. The first production of the project, "The Cancer Monologues," debuted in Santa Fe. Since then, the work has been created in other cities in the United States. Thompson's method requires using local stories in each production. The aim is to foster healing communities, not simply to provoke reaction through a few performances. "The Out Monologues" developed in the same way, with the performances being presented as an element of Santa Fe's Gay Pride celebration for the first time in 2005.

"When they first asked me about it, I said, 'Out?—I've never been in.' But then as we discussed it together, Jody and I realized that maybe we should participate." Their reasons were explained in an article in the June 17, 2005 Pasatiempo section of the *Santa Fe New Mexican*, that quoted Marcia. "Ordinarily if someone had asked us to participate in this project, we would have said no," said Muth. "But the climate in this country is so scary now. It reminds me of the McCarthy era. There's a feeling that we all have to be alike; we're turning into a cookie-cutter society and I don't like that. I especially don't like it in Santa Fe, where individuality was always encouraged. I want to let people know that we're just ordinary folks with the same desires and hopes as anybody else."

Their video-taped portion of the "Out Monologues" was played as part of the performance in mid-June, 2005 at the Armory for the Arts in Santa Fe. They attended and were warmly applauded by the entire audience. "We were really surprised and pleased to see people there that we knew from different areas of our lives—from Temple, from business, and other friends. We'd been a little concerned that there might be some of the parents of Jody's cello pupils who would be disturbed. But the only reaction from a parent was from a father who made a positive comment," Marcia said.

Another recognition for Marcia came in that same year. "I had never entered competition to be in a show since I'd begun painting. Jim encouraged me and of course, Jody did. So I thought I might as well do it. The show was going to be right here in town. Entering involved making a slide of the painting. Jim helped with that and when the slide was ready, I sent it off with the other necessary entry material. Later I got back the envelope in the mail one day. It was the same one I sent it in, so I almost didn't open it because I thought they were just returning the slide. Then I did open it and the letter began 'Congratulations,'" she said.

The show, Originals 2005, was a juried and invitational exhibition of New Mexico women artists organized by the New Mexico Committee of the National Museum of Women in the Arts in Washington, DC. The opening of the exhibit on September 23 featured a reception honoring the seventy-one juried artists and the three invitational artists. "We went to the opening. I watched to see people look at it, to see if they could relate to it. I noticed that they smiled when they stood there. It was hung in a very nice location. No one could miss it. I think people liked it because even if you didn't live in that time, you can relate to that little orchestra, people dancing, the food," Marcia said. "I have wondered why the judges selected it because it was not like anything else there," she said.

Pete Cecere, who lives in Woodville, Virginia, is a major collector of folk art who has several of Marcia's paintings. The first he acquired was *The Eviction of Adam and Eve.* Perhaps the judges saw the same thing he did in her work. His description was "quirkiness and mischievousness."

The painting that won her a place in that show, entitled *The Rally,* depicts an event in a Grange hall in the 1930s. The focus of the evening's festivities is a speech by a political candidate. But because the Grange hall was the center of Midwest rural community life, the occasion was also an excuse for music, food, and dancing. As in all of her memory paintings, the scene bursts with detail and the result is, as she said, something to which the viewer relates easily.

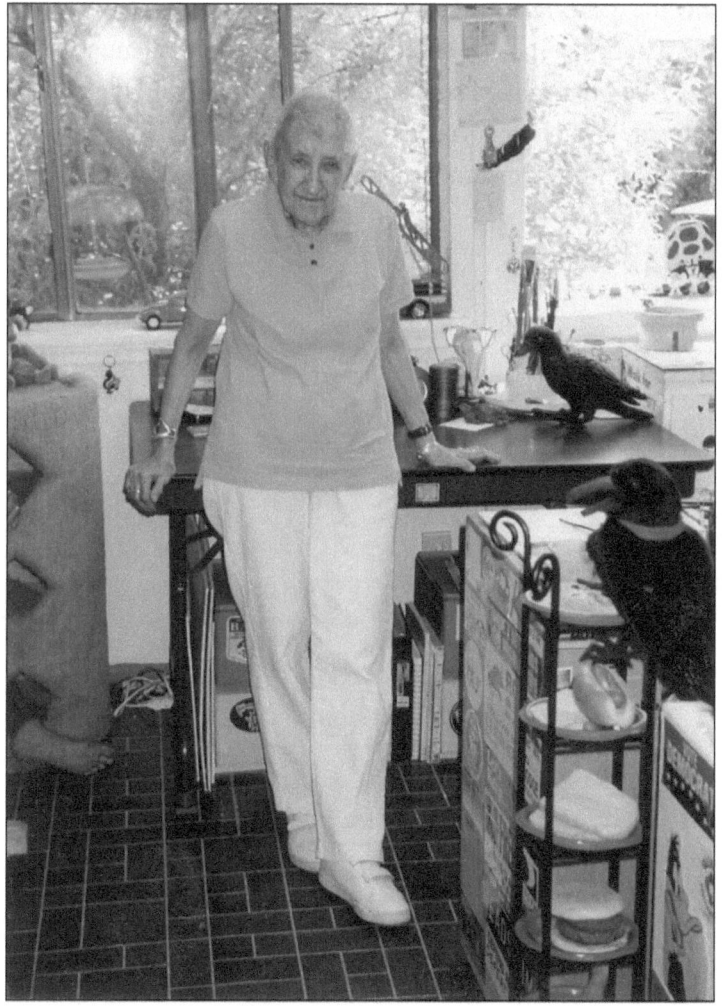

Marcia In Studio, 2005

"Someone called the other day and her husband talked to me. They had seen the exhibition. He said, 'You know, I just felt at home when I saw your painting because it was something I could understand.' I paint ordinary things," Marcia said.

True, the scenes are of ordinary people doing ordinary things, but Marcia Muth's interpretation is all her own. Asked if she could describe the criteria by which a painting is judged to be good, she replied, "There are basics such as composition that must be there, I suppose. But what makes someone decide a painting is good? There's really no way to know. If you like it and it says something to you, it's good." Setting her own standards, in life, in art, has worked for her for eighty-eight years.

Scene 20

Living Treasures

You carried your fate with you; it was your particular
accompanying genius. That's why translators of daimon
sometimes say "fate" and sometimes "genius," but never
"self." Hillman, J., *The Soul's Code*, p. 257
 We grow down, and we need a long life to get on
our feet. Hillman, J., *The Soul's Code*, p. 42

Months before the selection, friends and associates began writing letters of recommendation. Their intention was to convey the impact that Marcia Muth and Jody Ellis have had on them and on Santa Fe. The nominations probably included comments such as those in interviews for this book. Margeaux, a cello student of Jody's and a friend of both Marcia and Jody spoke of Marcia as an inspiration. "She's a person who wakes up each day surprised and open to it." Kay Lockridge said of Marcia that she is lively, challenging, bright and fun to be with. Those are adjectives one hears more often of the young than the elderly.

Roslyn Pulitzer spoke of Marcia and Jody, "The benefits of my acquaintance with both of them are almost too numerous to list. I've learned so much about Santa Fe and its people from both of them. I can read about the city and its history, but they have lived it. I always look forward to seeing them and come away with renewed vigor and enthusiasm for life."

The nominations were for Marcia and Jody to be selected as Santa Fe Living Treasures. The Living Treasures Program began in 1984. Since that time the honor has been bestowed on 175 Santa Fe citizens. The mission of the program is "to publicly honor elders (age 70 or older) who have generously served the community with kind hearts and good deeds. The oral histories of the honorees along with photographs are archived and made available to the public at the Fray Angelico Chavez History Library, Santa Fe, New Mexico."

A brochure from the organization explains the organization's history. "Peace activist and minister Mary Lou Cook, along with friends, founded the Santa Fe Living Treasures in 1984 . . . the group wanted to do something that wasn't being done—express appreciation for the important contributions of our Elders. In honoring them, the group aims to say a heartfelt 'Thank you' and to inspire others to become active in serving our community."

Those friends and colleagues who nominated Marcia and Jody must have wanted to find a public way to share their admiration for their lives. The aims of the Living Treasures Program were quite consistent with their desire to bring public honor to these two whom they admire. The result was that Marcia and Jody were two of the four Living Treasures named for 2006. The two others honored were Max Coll, who served as a New Mexico legislator for more than thirty years and Maralyn Budke, who served as chief of staff for two New Mexico governors.

An integral part of the Living Treasures program is collecting the oral histories that create a lasting record of the thoughts of those honored. Two interviewers visited Marcia and Jody in their home and recorded their recollections from their lives and their thoughts on several subjects. The recording became a part of the archive of the program, retained for posterity.

During the interview, Marcia was asked about her views of spirituality. "I believe that I am a child of God and as a child of God I have obligations. My idea of heaven is that one is in a position to help others. Maybe that's where some of my thoughts come from—someone doing that for me—from heaven." On the subject of four pieces of advice she would give to younger people interested in improving the world, she replied, "1. Learn history; 2. Religion can be divisive; 3. Do not hold resentments; 4. It's never too late to expand your creativity."

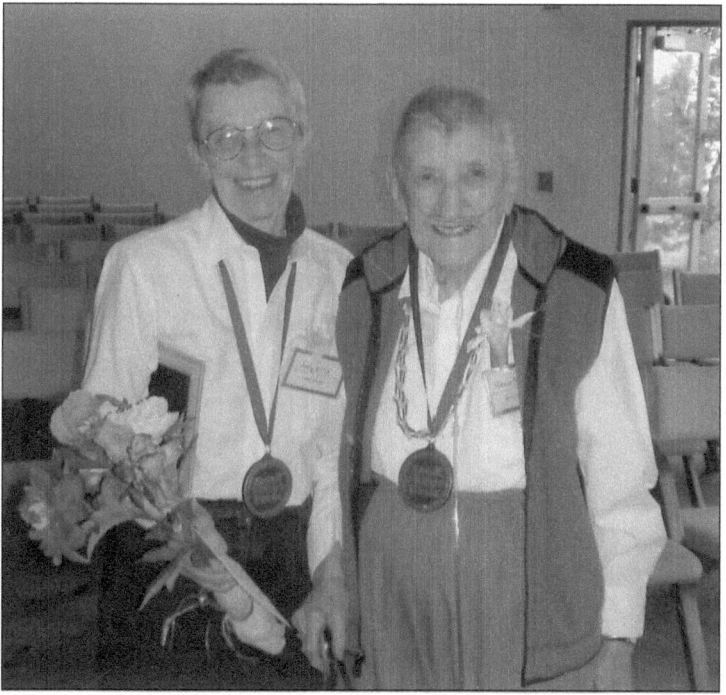

Jody Ellis and Marcia at Living Treasures Ceremony, 2006

As part of the ceremony Jim Smith presented Marcia and Jody each a medal that the Living Treasures program awards to its honorees. In addition to reading the medal's inscription, he said, "These two ladies are instrumental in my life."

Responding to the introduction, Marcia said, "This is quite an honor for someone who never grew up." Later, Marcia described the event as a very memorable and lovely ceremony. The applause that the honorees received that day was in the form of silent waves rather than applause, in deference to those in the audience who use hearing aids. The gratitude and warm wishes were more traditional in their expressions by those assembled.

Marcia and Jody also received a resolution from the Senate of the State of New Mexico. In addition to citing several accomplishments of each, the resolution stated " . . . together they have tried to promote compassion the best way they know how . . . and their unstoppable enthusiasm for art in general and Santa Fe in particular is a tribute to the beauty that surrounds them . . . ." In her acceptance comments, Marcia said, "Just remember, don't fear getting older. Getting older just means you have more time to explore and enhance your creativity and share it with others."

They were named Living Treasures as a couple and both their individual and collective endeavors were mentioned in their introductions that day. Although for some, they have become an inseparable unit, both Marcia and Jody retain their individuality.

≒ ≒ ≒

These scenes from Marcia's life in this book suggest something of how her *daimon* has helped shape that individuality and affected her path. These scenes do not tell an entire life history. Even if that had been intended, Marcia could not have allowed it. "I am not an unwilling subject, but I am a sometimes reluctant one. There are some things that

I don't tell," she said. Instead, collectively these scenes are an exhibition, a one woman show, illustrating points in that history.

Hillman wrote "... we need a long life to get on our feet." There's no description in his work of a specific end point to the growing down that some are fortunate to do. Marcia Muth seems to still be working on the process: "giving back what circumstance gave her by means of gestures that declare her full attachment to this world."

That, she doesn't have to tell. It is evident.

www.ingramcontent.com/pod-product-compliance
Lightning Source LLC
Chambersburg PA
CBHW030744180526
45163CB00003B/915